BUYING WATERFRONT PROPERTY IN MICHIGAN

By Clifford H. Bloom

For information, please contact
Michigan Lake & Stream Associations, Inc.,
306 E. Main St., Stanton, Michigan 48888
or call (989) 831-5100.

Printed and bound in the United States

ISBN 978-0-615-51123-8

CONTENTS

ATTACHMENTS

INTRODUCTION

BUYING OR SELLING REAL PROPERTY IS A TRANSACTION
that should always be approached very carefully, deliberately,
and methodically. Any real estate transaction can involve many
potential pitfalls. That is especially true regarding the sale or
purchase of waterfront property, whether the property is located at
an inland lake, one of the Great Lakes, a pond, or a river, stream, or
creek.

This book is intended to be a general "how-to" practical guide for
anyone who is considering buying or selling waterfront property
in Michigan. Of course, no publication can take the place of real
life experience as well as retaining the services of one or more real
estate professionals. In addition, given the many issues typically
involved with a waterfront property, as well as the normally high
monetary sums associated with such properties, it is almost always
prudent to utilize the services of a qualified real estate attorney and
real estate professional (such as a realtor or real estate agent). This
publication does not constitute the giving of legal, accounting, or
similar advice or counsel.

Although we have strived to be accurate in the matters contained
in this publication, this book is provided for informational

I would like to thank the Michigan Lake & Stream Associations, Inc. ("ML&SA") for its sponsorship of this book. In particular, the assistance I received from Carol McVicker, Sharon Wagner and Scott Brown of ML&SA was invaluable. I would also like to thank Elaine Kitchel, Crystal Morgan, and David Caldon of Law Weathers for their assistance with the production of this book. In addition, I owe a debt of gratitude to Bob Larson, a professional real estate appraiser (of R.J. Larson Appraisals) of Grand Rapids, Michigan, Kerene Morrissey of Reinhart Realtors, Chelsea, Michigan and Mark Riggle of the Riggle Team-RE/MAX Irish Hills Realtors, Manitou Beach, Michigan for reviewing a draft of this work and making valuable comments in order to improve the final version of this publication. I would also like to thank Dr. Niles Kevern, professor emeritus, Michigan State University Department of Fisheries and Wildlife for his insightful comments and suggestions in improving this book.

Finally, I would like to thank all of the riparians out there who have attended my many seminars on riparian issues, supported my regular column in *The Michigan Riparian* magazine, read my other publications, and have generally been very supportive over the years.

— Clifford H. Bloom
Attorney at Law

Chapter 1
THE PITFALLS

ISN'T BUYING AND SELLING WATERFRONT PROPERTY in Michigan virtually the same as purchasing or selling any other real estate? Absolutely not! There are many issues associated with waterfront properties in Michigan that are not present with other real estate. Anyone who does not appreciate (and plan for) those differences regarding a purchase or sales transaction involving a waterfront property does so at their own significant risk.

The differences between the sales of waterfront properties versus other properties begins prior to the signing of a purchase/ sales agreement for the property, extends through the "due diligence" process (both before the purchase/sales agreement is signed and prior to closing) and through (and even after) closing. While on the surface many of the general steps for buying and selling waterfront property appear to be the same as for nonwaterfront properties (for example, signing a purchase/sales agreement, proceeding through the contingencies in that agreement, securing financing, reviewing the title insurance commitment before closing, and proceeding to closing), there really are vast differences.

Some of the issues associated with waterfront real estate transactions that are usually not present with other real property transactions include, but are not limited to, the following:

- Is the property truly waterfront (riparian)? Or is there a "land gap" between the parcel and the water?
- What are the property owner's riparian rights (and the limits thereof)?
- Are there applicable deed restrictions or restrictive covenants?
- If a vacant property, is it "buildable"?
- Are there any lake access devices on the property involved or adjacent to the property that may create problems (for example, lake access easements, road ends, parks, alleys, walkways, etc.)?
- Is there a lake or riverfront property owners association, and if so, is it mandatory? Are there dues or assessments?
- Are there any special assessments regarding the body of water (or otherwise) that bind the property? Is there a statutory lake board?
- Is the waterfront and body of water healthy and clean, or degraded and potentially polluted?
- Are the shoreline and bottomlands for the property desirable or problematic (muddy, erosion-prone, etc.)?
- Are there any claims to the parcel (on dry land or out along the shore or bottomlands) by the neighboring property owner(s), such as adverse possession or prescriptive easement rights? Do any boundary line disputes or problems exist?
- Does the water level vary dramatically? Is the water level ever so high as to cause flooding or so low as to impair enjoyment of the waterfront? Is there a dam that regulates water levels?
- Has a formal lake water level been established?
- Is the cottage or dwelling (or any other structures or improvements) located within a floodplain or flood zone? That may significantly affect homeowner's insurance premiums as well as implicate many other issues.
- Are there wetlands issues?
- How much waterfront does the parcel really have?
- Can the existing dwelling be replaced or added onto under the local zoning regulations?

- Was the property ever "filled" such that settling might be a real problem if a dwelling is built or expanded?

- Are there any local municipal regulations regarding dock limitations, swim rafts, seawalls, the number of watercraft allowed, or similar matters?

- Who owns the adjacent bottomlands, at what angles, and where are the limits?

You get the picture. Waterfront properties often have "issues."

Chapter 2
IS THE PROPERTY TRULY WATERFRONT AND RIPARIAN?

A KEY ISSUE REGARDING THE PURCHASE OR SALE OF a waterfront property in Michigan is whether or not the property is truly waterfront or riparian. That seems like a fairly simple question to answer, but that is not always the case.

Technically, in Michigan, a property that touches or has frontage on a lake (whether an inland lake or one of the Great Lakes) is "littoral." Properties touching or having frontage on a flowing body of water, such as a river, creek, or stream, are "riparian." Nevertheless, the word "riparian" has been commonly used for years to refer to any property fronting on or touching any body of water (whether a lake, stream, river, or creek, but not a wetland or pond), such that even the Michigan courts typically refer to all such properties as "riparian."[1] See *Glass v Goeckel*, 473 Mich 667; 703 NW2d 58 (2005); *Thies v Howland*, 424 Mich 282; 380 NW2d 463 (1985); *Thompson v Enz*, 379 Mich 667; 154 NW2d 473 (1967). Accordingly, in this book, unless expressly indicated otherwise, the word "riparian" shall refer to property fronting on any body of water, except ponds or wetlands. "Riparian" is sometimes also used to refer to the owner of a riparian or waterfront property.

In Michigan, property that touches or fronts on a body of water is riparian. See *Thies v Howland*, 424 Mich 282; 380 NW2d 463

(1985); *Rice v Naimish*, 8 Mich App 698; 155 NW2d 370 (1967); *Hall v Wantz*, 336 Mich 112; 57 NW2d 462 (1953); *Hess v West Bloomfield Twp*, 439 Mich 550; 486 NW2d 628 (1992). Conversely, property that does not touch or front on a body of water is not riparian.[2] See *Thompson v Enz*, 379 Mich 667; 154 NW2d 473 (1967); *Little v Kin*, 249 Mich App 502; 644 NW2d 375 (2002); *aff'd in part and reversed in part*, 468 Mich 699; 664 NW2d 749 (2003). Unfortunately, that simple concept is often misunderstood. Nonriparian properties (often referred to as off-water properties or "backlots") can have access to a body of water pursuant to a number of lake access devices such as private easements across riparian properties, road ends, parks, outlots, walks, alleys, and community beaches. Sometimes, those lake access devices are "public" (whereby any member of the public can utilize the lake access device, not just nearby backlot property owners), while other lake access devices are "private" (limited to the use of certain or all backlot property owners). In either case, those backlots are not "riparian" simply because they have access to a nearby lake, river, or stream. Even in those cases where an easement accords a backlot expressly written enumerated rights almost equal to those of a riparian property owner, the backlot property owner still is not a riparian. See *Little v Kin*, 249 Mich App 502; 644 NW2d 375 (2002); aff'd in part and reversed in part, 468 Mich 699; 664 NW2d 749 (2003); *Dyball v Lennox*, 260 Mich App 698; 680 NW2d 522 (2004); *Thies v Howland*, 424 Mich 282; 380 NW2d 463 (1985).

For properties adjacent to the waterfront, isn't it easy to ascertain whether or not a particular property is "riparian" simply by reviewing the legal description, the original plat (if it is a platted lot), or a survey? Unfortunately, it is not always that simple. In some cases, the property appears to be waterfront (or at least an apparently unencumbered waterfront), only to have it turn out later that there is a property "gap" between the parcel or lot involved and the water that is owned by someone else. Or, situations arise where there is a platted road, walk, park, or land strip located between the body of water and the lot or parcel involved. It is not uncommon for a person who purchased what they believed to be an unencumbered waterfront property to have a rude awakening later when a shoreline "gap" is discovered or members of the public or backlot owners in the plat involved start utilizing the shoreline of the property with the full support of Michigan law due to the presence of a previously-forgotten dedicated easement, road right-of-way, walk, park, or alley located between the purchaser's new lot and the water.

Such waterfront problems tend to fall into one of two categories. First, situations arise where the lot or property involved does not actually extend to the water's edge (and as such, is not riparian). There is a "land gap" between the lot and the water. The second situation involves the above-mentioned so-called "parallel" easements or lake access devices benefiting the public or other lot owners within the plat such as an easement, road right-of-way, park, walkway, or alley. These items often run along the waterfront. The parcel or lot may still be riparian or waterfront, but subject to usage rights of others. Please see Chapter 33 of this book for a more in-depth discussion of waterfront access devices.

In Michigan, legal descriptions for waterfront properties almost never expressly extend beyond the water's edge or shoreline and rarely describe the bottomlands of a body of water.[3] In fact, legal descriptions for waterfront property in Michigan almost never expressly state that the property involved is riparian. In almost all cases, however, where a bona fide legal description in the chain of title for a particular property describes the property as "extending to the water's edge," "ending at the water's edge," "going to the water's edge," "extending along the water's edge," "running along the shore," "going to the lake (or river)," or similar language, it means that the property is riparian. Furthermore, Michigan courts generally interpret that language on inland lakes as meaning that the bottomlands adjacent to that property are also included within the legal description, even though the legal description indicates or implies that the property "ends" at the water's edge. See *Hilt v Weber*, 252 Mich 198; 233 NW 159 (1930); *Mumaugh v McCarley*, 219 Mich App 641; 558 NW2d 433 (1996); *Bauman v Barendregt*, 251 Mich 67; 231 NW 70 (1930). Of course, such language does not rule out the presence of an easement, road right-of-way, etc., along the waterfront that must be ferreted out by the due diligence of the prospective purchaser.

What is a "meander line"? Despite popular misconceptions, it is generally <u>not</u> a boundary line or an indication of specifically where a lakefront lot ends or the water was located when the lot or parcel was created. A meander line is often defined as a traverse of the margin of a permanent natural body of water. The original government surveys for properties in Michigan (from 150 years ago or even earlier) often used meander lines to ascertain the amount of dry land remaining after separating out the water area. Normally, the lake, river, or stream itself determines boundary lines, not meander lines.

What is a "traverse line"? A traverse line is a technique used by surveyors to describe an area along a lake or shoreline, without having to actually survey every nook and cranny along an irregular shoreline. Typically, a surveyor will legally describe a traverse line that is slightly landward of the body of water, and then indicate that the legal description for the lot or parcel also includes all property located between the traverse line and the body of water.

Footnotes

[1] Ponds and some artificial lakes may not have riparian rights. See *Persell v Wertz*, 287 Mich App 576 (2010); *In Re Martiny Lakes Project*, 381 Mich 180; 160 NW2d 909 (1968); *Thompson v Enz*, 379 Mich 667; 154 NW2d 473 (1967).

[2] William Shakespeare's phrase "a rose by any other name would smell as sweet" clearly does not apply!

[3] And, in fact, this can create a real problem regarding the apportionment of bottom-lands—that is, which waterfront property owner owns which bottomlands.

Chapter 3
CHARACTERISTICS AND RIGHTS OF RIPARIAN PROPERTY

WHAT LEGAL RIGHTS DOES A RIPARIAN PROPERTY owner enjoy? Normally, a riparian has the right of enjoyment attendant to all lawful uses which can be made of the lakefront. Such rights include swimming, fishing, hunting, boating, and other recreational uses. See *Thies v Howland*, 424 Mich 282; 380 NW2d 463 (1985); *Burt v Munger*, 314 Mich 659; 23 NW2d 117 (1946); *Hilt v Weber*, 252 Mich 198; 233 NW 159 (1930); *Pierce v Riley*, 81 Mich App 39; 264 NW2d 110 (1978); *Sewers v Hacklander*, 219 Mich 143; 188 NW 547 (1922); *Hall v Alford*, 114 Mich 165; 72 NW 137 (1897). Riparians have the exclusive right to install and utilize one or more docks, boat hoists, or boat cradles, swim rafts, and similar items along their water frontage. Riparians also have the right to permanently moor one or more boats and watercraft along their lakefront and bottomlands.[4]

In addition to the normal recreational riparian rights, a riparian also has the legal right to draw water from a body of water for irrigation and similar purposes. See *Thompson v Enz*, 379 Mich 667; 154 NW2d 473 (1967); *Schenk v Ann Arbor*, 196 Mich 75; 163 NW 109 (1917); *Hoover v Crane*, 362 Mich 36; 106 NW2d 563 (1960). A riparian even has the right to draw water from a body of water or the ground and to sell that water subject to the "reasonable use" doctrine. See *Anglers of the Au Sable, Inc v Mich Dept of*

Environmental Quality, 283 Mich App 115; 770 NW2d 359 (2009); *aff'd in part and rev'd in part*, 488 Mich 69 (2010).

The usage rights of a riparian property owner in Michigan are not unlimited, however. Riparian rights are subject to both common law and legislative (or ordinance) limitations. Michigan has a common law doctrine often referred to as the "reasonable use" doctrine (also called the "riparian rights" doctrine). That rule indicates that a riparian property owner cannot utilize his or her riparian rights in a fashion that unreasonably interferes with the riparian rights of other riparian property owners. See *Thompson v Enz*, 379 Mich 667; 154 NW2d 473 (1967); *Three Lakes Assn v Kessler*, 91 Mich App 371; 285 NW2d 300 (1979); *Pierce v Riley*, 81 Mich App 39; 264 NW2d 110 (1978); *West Michigan Dock & Market Corp v Lakeland Investments*, 210 Mich App 505; 534 NW2d 212 (1995), and *Square Lake Hills Condo Assn v Bloomfield Twp*, 437 Mich 310; 471 NW2d 321 (1991). For example, a riparian property owner cannot install a dock on his/her bottomlands that extends so far out into the lake that it interferes with navigability or the reasonable boating activities of other riparian property owners. Nor can a developer create a development and "funnel" so many new homeowners onto a lake through a limited lake frontage property as to unreasonably overcrowd the lake or unreasonably interfere with the lawful uses of adjoining riparian property owners. *Ibid.*

In addition to potential common law limitations, the rights of a riparian property owner are also subject to regulation under state law (for example, Michigan statutes regulate such topics as wetlands alterations, building in and near sand dune areas, permanent docks, dredging in the water, and sanding beaches) and local regulations (for example, local zoning regulations, dock ordinances, and other ordinances).

What about bottomlands ownership? It depends upon whether the property abuts an inland lake, one of the Great Lakes, or a river. For most inland lakes in Michigan, a riparian property owner owns the bottomlands adjacent to his/her lakefront property and out to the center of the lake. See *Hall v Wantz*, 336 Mich 112; 57 NW2d 462 (1953); *Gregory v LaFaive*, 172 Mich App 354; 431 NW2d 511 (1988); *West Michigan Dock & Market Corp v Lakeland Investment*, 210 Mich App 505; 534 NW2d 212 (1995). For a round lake, each riparian landowner would own a "pie-shaped" piece of bottomlands radiating to a point in the center of the lake. Unfortunately, however, there are very few round (or nearly round) lakes in Michigan. Accordingly, the Michigan courts have resorted to several different methods for allocating bottomlands on irregular inland lakes in Michigan. In most cases, the courts draw a "thread" or line (which can be straight or gyrating) in the center (or centers) of the lake, to which the bottomlands of various properties radiate. See *Heeringa v Petroelje*, 279 Mich App 444; 760 NW2d 538 (2008); *Weisenburger v Kirkwood*, 7 Mich App 283; 151 NW2d 889 (1979). As more than one judge has noted, determining the riparian boundary lines under a lake in order to allocate bottomlands is more of an art than a science.

Why would a riparian property owner need to know the exact location of his/her bottomland boundaries under the lake? Given that many riparian lots or parcels on inland lakes in Michigan are relatively small, riparian or lake frontage space is at a premium. Sometimes, a riparian property owner needs to know where his/her riparian boundary lines are located under the water in order to determine dock placement, where an aquatic raft can be anchored, and similar matters. In Michigan, the only person who can install a dock, anchor an aquatic raft, or permanently moor boats over specific bottomlands is the owner of those bottomlands (or someone else with that landowner's permission).

Although many surveyors claim to be able to perform riparian boundary (bottomlands) surveys, few surveyors have the expertise or experience to do them well. Engineers who do surveying work are often more qualified to perform authoritative riparian boundary line surveys. In the end, however, only a Michigan court can definitively determine riparian boundary lines. Any riparian boundary line survey done by a surveyor or engineer is simply a nonbinding opinion (similar to a legal opinion by an attorney).

The rule for bottomlands ownership is different for the Great Lakes. For most Michigan properties located on one of the Great Lakes, the riparian landowner owns a "movable fee" down to the edge of the water. See *Glass v Goeckel*, 473 Mich 667; 703 NW2d 58 (2005); *Hilt v Weber*, 252 Mich 198; 233 NW 159 (1930); *Mumaugh v McCarley*, 219 Mich App 641; 558 NW2d 433 (1996). In some portions of the Great Lakes, the movable property line (the water's edge) can literally change by many feet overnight. The property covered by the waters of the Great Lakes is owned by the people of the state of Michigan. Adjoining riparian landowners do not own any of the water-covered bottomlands of the Great Lakes. However, when those bottomlands are "exposed," the riparian

Great Lakes landowner typically does "own" or at least control those exposed bottomlands, at least temporarily. Some Michigan case law implies that a riparian landowner on the Great Lakes probably does not "own" the exposed bottomlands below (or lakeside) of the ordinary high water mark of the Great Lakes. That case law seems to indicate, however, that a riparian landowner does "control" exposed bottomlands below the ordinary high water mark and can exercise domain over those exposed bottomlands to the exclusion of others and members of the public (except for the public trust navigability easement mentioned below). See the Michigan Great Lakes Submerged Lands Act, MCL 324.32501 *et seq.* and Michigan Attorney General Opinion No. 5327 (July 6, 1978).

Another unique aspect of Great Lakes riparian lands involves an invisible permanent easement for navigability for "public trust doctrine" purposes. The Michigan Supreme Court in *Glass v Goeckel*, 473 Mich 667; 703 NW2d 58 (2005), held that all private riparian properties on the Great Lakes in Michigan are subject to an invisible public easement up to the ordinary high water mark of the property involved for "navigability." In the context of the *Glass v Goeckel* decision, that means that members of the public can walk (without permission) along the shore of any private riparian property on the Great Lakes in Michigan up to the ordinary high water mark. This public easement for navigability (travel) is imposed by law and does not show up in any recorded document in a title search. The easement is limited, however. It is highly unlikely that members of the public could sunbathe, lounge, camp, or engage in similar nontravel uses on the shoreline of private properties on the Great Lakes "below" (lakeward of) the ordinary high water mark without the permission of the riparian landowner.[5]

Bottomland ownership and use rules in Michigan are slightly different for a stream or river than a lake. A flowing body of water is often referred to as a "watercourse," which can constitute a river, stream, or creek. In general, lakes and watercourses are treated similarly with regard to bottomlands ownership. A riparian property owner normally owns to the center "thread" of a flowing body of water, unless the riparian landowner owns both sides of the stream, creek, or river or the original legal descriptions indicate otherwise. Larger bodies of flowing waters tends to be "navigable," while smaller ones are generally not navigable. Navigability allows the public access to the body of water involved, including the ability to wade on the bottomlands thereof.

Footnotes

[4] Michigan case law is sometimes confusing in that it indicates that members of the public have the right to swim, fish, boat, etc., on Michigan bodies of water. However, that is only true if the members of the public lawfully gain access to the body of water. If a member of the public cannot lawfully gain access to a body of water, that person cannot lawfully engage in those uses. In addition, those uses can only be engaged in once the person is on the surface of the water. On inland lakes and non-navigable streams, using the bottomlands of another without the riparian property owner's permission can constitute a trespass. See *Swartz v Sherston*, 299 Mich 423; 300 NW 148 (1941); *Hilt v Weber*, 252 Mich 198; 233 NW 159 (1930); *Hall v Wantz*, 336 Mich 112; 57 NW2d 462 (1953).

[5] Exactly where the common law ordinary high water mark is located on a given riparian property is often problematic.

Chapter 4
BENEFITS OF PURCHASING A RIPARIAN PROPERTY

OF COURSE, VIRTUALLY EVERYONE WOULD LIKE TO either live on or own a second home at a lake, river, or stream. Sadly, for most people, that dream is never realized. For the lucky few who become riparians at some point in time during their lives, the riparian experience is almost always extremely rewarding.

Michigan is not referred to as the "Water Wonderland" or the "Great Lakes State" for nothing! Part of the magic of Michigan is not only the bordering Great Lakes, but also the numerous inland lakes, rivers, streams, and waterways. Who could forget their childhood trips to Mackinac Island, Tahquamenon Falls, or the Soo Locks?[6] Many Michiganders have camped, swam, or sunbathed at waterfront state parks throughout Michigan, such as South Haven, Holland, Pentwater, Grand Haven, Wilderness, Silver Lake, or Bay City. Many tourists have spent time enjoying lakefront cities, such as Ludington, Port Huron, Cedarville, Munising, Saugatuck, Petoskey, Traverse City, Charlevoix, Cheboygan, and Alpena. There are countless cottages, cabins, homes, and beachfront dwellings on inland lakes throughout Michigan. Hunters and fishermen have enjoyed using waterfront property at many locations throughout Michigan, including on the Grand River, Au Sable River, Pine River, Pere Marquette River, Manistee River, Big Two Hearted River, and Fox River. Who hasn't fallen in love with Michigan islands such as Mackinac, Beaver, Drummond, North Manitou, or Grand? It seems as if Michiganders can rarely get enough of their waterfront recreational activities.

Over the long run, owning waterfront property in Michigan has, with few exceptions, been a relatively good investment. Except for several severe economic downturns, waterfront properties in Michigan generally appreciate in value on an annual basis. During economic downturns, waterfront property frequently does not devalue, and in those cases where even waterfront property values are hit, it generally means merely a "stall" in valuation appreciation or a light drop in property value during the downturn, which is almost always less severe than the actual devaluation of nonwaterfront properties.

Some of the other benefits of owning waterfront property include the following:

- The obvious recreational opportunities, which include boating, swimming, water skiing, ice sports, kayaking, fishing, and general recreation.
- Diminishment of the need for renting waterfront vacation property or vacationing elsewhere.
- Becoming a member of a fairly select group—riparians.
- Having a great venue to entertain family and friends.
- Lake neighborhoods are typically close-knit communities with many opportunities for socializing, making new friends, and being part of an integral community.
- Being a riparian often encourages the person to become more conservation-minded and environmentally aware and active.
- Waterfront properties are normally easier to sell quickly than nonriparian properties if the need arises.
- Viewing more wildlife such as geese, swans, ducks, loons, eagles, muskrats, and beavers.

Footnotes

[6] Despite popular myth to the contrary, the Upper Peninsula is still a part of Michigan, both geographically and legally! Accordingly, all of the rules and matters contained in this book that apply to the Lower Peninsula of Michigan (and all those living "below" the Mackinaw Bridge) also apply to the Upper Peninsula and those living there (self-proclaimed "Yoopers").

Chapter 5
DISADVANTAGES OF OWNING WATERFRONT PROPERTY

OF COURSE, WHILE BEING A RIPARIAN IS GENERALLY a very positive experience, there are some drawbacks. Those drawbacks can include the following:

- Waterfront properties command a premium price, and are beyond the financial reach of most people.

- Property taxes tend to be higher for waterfront properties, although the "caps" associated with property taxes under Proposal A have minimized some of those negative tax impacts, particularly if one owns a waterfront property for a long period of time.

- Cherished waterfront properties often can pose difficult estate planning and family succession issues.

- Waterfront properties can create friction between neighbors. This is particularly true where a waterfront neighborhood has lots or parcels that are relatively small, such that the actual water frontage is limited for each lot or parcel. Problems such as boundary line disputes, adverse possession or prescriptive easement claims, dock placement issues, noise, the coming and going of power boats, sharing a private road, and similar matters can create tension and friction between waterfront neighbors.

- Waterfront properties often entail more upkeep and work than nonriparian properties. Examples include putting in docks, boats, boat lifts, and similar items during the spring and taking them out in the fall, raking dead aquatic weeds from the shore, winterizing and storing boats during the off season, and repairing and maintaining boats and other water "toys."

- There are heightened dangers associated with the waterfront such as drowning, falling through the ice in the winter, and high-speed boating or water skiing accidents.

- Even apart from the high purchase price for a waterfront property, there are additional expenses that are generally incurred which are not applicable to nonwaterfront properties. Those costs can include aquatic weed treatments, seawalls, the purchase and upkeep of boats and other water toys, landscaping between the dwelling and the lake, lake association dues, and additional insurance.

- Since the lake, river, or stream is owned and shared in common with other property owners, conflicts frequently arise.

- Many of the laws and rights associated with riparian ownership are not well understood by lay people, law enforcement officials, and on occasion, even some attorneys and judges.

- Riparian properties that have public or backlot access devices such as easements, road ends, parallel roads, parks, etc., located on them or nearby can cause severe headaches for the riparian landowner.

- Many waterfronts involve small lots with cramped neighborhoods and limited parking.

- Maintaining the waterfront (gathering and disposing of dead aquatic leaves and weeds, raking beaches, etc.) can be frustrating.

- Many riparian properties are located on private roads or old, substandard public roads where upkeep, safety, and parking can be a problem.

Chapter 6
DUE DILIGENCE

"DUE DILIGENCE" CAN BE DEFINED AS PROCEEDING with caution, the care exercised by a person who seeks to satisfy a legal requirement, or a prospective buyer's investigation and analysis of a piece of property before finally purchasing the same. Or put another way, "due diligence" is a diligent and careful investigative process.

There are generally two types of due diligence that are applicable to the purchase or sale of a waterfront property. First, there is due diligence that must be done <u>before</u> a purchase/sales agreement for a particular waterfront lot or parcel is signed. Second, there is a due diligence period between the time that a purchase/sales agreement is signed and the closing (*i.e.,* the exchanging of money for a deed or land contract) occurs. This interim time period is very important.

Pursuing proper due diligence is particularly important when buying or selling a waterfront property. For such properties, the pitfalls can be extreme if important matters are missed or proper procedures are not followed.

Chapter 7
DUE DILIGENCE BEFORE THE PURCHASE/SALES AGREEMENT IS SIGNED

THERE ARE TWO GENERAL STEPS FOR THE PURCHASE or sale of a waterfront property. First, the purchase/sales agreement is signed by the prospective purchaser. Second, and sometime thereafter, the "closing" occurs. The closing can be defined as the final step in a real estate purchase/sales transaction. It is the final meeting between the buyer and seller at which the transaction is consummated (normally, where the conveyance or title documents are exchanged and the money and property are transferred). The closing could also be considered the final settlement of the real estate transaction. The first due diligence period is <u>before</u> the purchase/sales agreement is signed. The second due diligence period is the time between the signing of the purchase/sales agreement and closing. Please see Attachment A for a helpful "due diligence" checklist.

Perhaps the biggest mistake that a prospective buyer or purchaser of a waterfront property can make with regard to the purchase/sales agreement is the erroneous lay person's assumption that the written purchase/sales agreement is some type of nonbinding, preliminary letter of intent that can be disregarded or modified later if necessary. That is almost always <u>never</u> the case. In almost all situations, an executed purchase/sales agreement for real estate is a <u>fully binding contract</u>, which cannot be modified, changed, or varied without the express written consent of both parties. And, quite often, the party on the other side will not agree to an amendment or change.

It is true that most purchase/sales agreements for real estate do contain several contingency clauses, such that one party or the other can potentially cancel the contract if a contingency is not met. Nevertheless, the purchase/sales agreement is still a binding contract and if all of the contingencies (or "out" clauses) are met, the closing must occur. Just because such an agreement contains contingencies does not mean that it is not a binding contract.

Given the binding nature of a purchase/sales agreement for waterfront property, it is <u>very</u> important that each party do their own due diligence <u>before</u> signing the agreement. Each party must make certain that they are willing to live with all of the terms of the purchase/sales agreement before it is signed.

Some of the matters that a prospective purchaser of a waterfront property should pursue as part of "due diligence" <u>before</u> a purchase/sales agreement for the property is signed include the following:

- Retain the assistance of a qualified realtor, real estate agent, real estate broker, and/or real estate attorney.

- Negotiate all terms and phrases within the proposed purchase/sales agreement (and make certain that you understand them). Also, make sure that the final written agreement accurately reflects what has been agreed to.

- Insert all desired contingency clauses into the purchase/sales agreement.

- Investigate all matters to your satisfaction that will not be subject to a contingency clause in the purchase/sales agreement.

- Satisfy yourself that you can secure proper financing.

An additional useful "Buyer's Checklist" is included as Attachment B.

Chapter 8
THE ALL-IMPORTANT PURCHASE/SALES AGREEMENT

WITH THE EXCEPTION OF PERHAPS THE DEED (OR land contract) and the title insurance policy, the purchase/sales agreement is probably the most important document in a waterfront sales transaction. A sample purchase/sales agreement can be found in Attachment C. A purchase/sales agreement is a binding contract. It is not merely a guide, letter of intent, or other nonbinding document. Unless both the prospective buyer and seller agree to a formal signed written amendment or change to an already-signed purchase/sales agreement, both parties are "stuck" with the originally-executed purchase/sales agreement.

All of the significant terms of the property purchase/sale should be expressly dealt with in the purchase/sales agreement. Many of the important items to be covered by the agreement are listed in Attachment D. Some of those important items include, but are not limited to, a preface or introductory clause that often states the names and addresses of the parties and the purpose of the agreement or contract, a "time is of the essence" clause, environmental issues, a risk of loss clause, an "as-is" clause for the seller (no warranties except as to title) or an express warranty, the purchase price, legal description for the property, fixtures and personal items included in the sale (full or partial "with contents" clause), financing, earnest money deposit, who pays any broker or expert fees, proration of property taxes at closing, proration for other fees (water bills, association dues, etc.), the type of deed or land contract to be given at closing, title warranties, representations, miscellaneous contingencies, real estate transfer taxes, arbitration clause, possession date, the closing date, seller's disclosure, land division rights (if any), survey, inspections, closing costs, title insurance (and title commitment), and remedies upon a breach. Unlike most purchase/sales agreements, however, a purchase/sales agreement for riparian property may also include a representation and warranty on behalf of the seller, or a contingency allowing the buyer to confirm, that the property includes not less than a specified number of feet of frontage on a particular body of water.

In Michigan, to be valid, an agreement regarding the purchase or sale of real property must be in a written document, signed by both parties. This is covered by what is commonly called the "Statute of Frauds." See MCL 566.106, 556.108, and 556.132. Every contract in Michigan must include an offer and an acceptance. *Mathieu v Wubbe*, 330 Mich 408 (1951). In a real estate purchase/sales agreement, typically, the buyer makes the "offer" and the seller effectuates an "acceptance." Once the purchase/sales agreement has been signed by the parties, it is not really that important who made the "offer" and who made the "acceptance." At a bare minimum, a binding purchase/sales agreement for real estate in Michigan must be in writing and must include the following essential terms:

- A description of the property (address, permanent parcel number/tax identification number, and/or the actual legal description).
- The terms (including the purchase price, which is sometimes called the "consideration").
- The time of performance.
- It must be signed by both parties.

While no one wants to make the purchase of a waterfront property any more adversarial than the transaction needs to be, a prospective purchaser should assume that no representation, warranty, promise, agreement, or guarantee by the seller (or the seller's realtor, broker, or attorney) is binding unless it has been put in writing and signed by the seller. The notion that the buyer and seller can have side oral agreements will frequently involve promises or representations that prove forgotten or unenforceable.

If a purchase/sales agreement is litigated in court and there is an ambiguity, Michigan law indicates that any ambiguity is to be construed against the party who drafted the document, which is usually the seller (although sometimes it is the buyer). If there is a standard printed purchase/sales agreement provided by the seller, generally any ambiguity will be construed against the seller. *Cousins v Melvin F Lanphar & Co*, 312 Mich 715 (1945); *Keller v Paulos Land Co*, 381 Mich 355 (1968).

In Michigan, there is no legal requirement that a specific form or type of a purchase/sales agreement be utilized (although certain wording or topics must be included in the written document). Typically, real estate brokers have come up with standard purchase/sales agreement forms for different regions of Michigan, which are generally widely accepted. There are other forms available. On occasion, the parties themselves (or their attorneys) will draft a unique contract for the particular real estate transaction involved. Whenever standard forms are used, they will likely require some modification—even "good" forms must usually be altered. Regardless of whether a standard or customized form is used, both parties should fully and carefully read all portions of the agreement and understand all terms <u>before</u> signing. Better yet, whether you are a buyer or a seller, have your real estate attorney review the document before you sign it. Do not assume that the document can be modified later. Typically, the document cannot be amended unless the other side also agrees in writing, which frequently, the other side will refuse to do.

Of course, the most important term in any purchase/sales agreement is likely to be the price of the property. Realtors and real estate agents typically have extensive experience in determining realistic property sales prices. They also have access to a significant number of databases that will help the seller determine a reasonable listing price, as well as advising buyers what a particular property is really worth. Under Michigan law, the assessed value of a property should equal 50 percent of the true cash value (or fair market value) of the property. Thus, theoretically, doubling the assessed value or state equalized value of a property (not the "taxable value") should provide a fairly good indication of what the property is worth. Finally, either a buyer or seller can hire an independent third-party appraiser to give a formal professional opinion regarding what the property is worth.

Quite often, a "mating ritual" occurs between a seller and a potential buyer regarding the proposed purchase/sales agreement.

One party (or the other) will submit a purchase/sales agreement to the other side (with specific terms and conditions), which will be rejected by the receiving party. That party will then submit a new revised purchase/sales agreement or a written counter-offer. That counter-offer is sometimes rejected and the first party will submit a counter-counter-proposal. In some situations, such "back and forth" can be a waste of time. In many cases, it is best for the parties to simply agree orally on the significant terms (such as the purchase price and financing), with one of the parties then preparing a purchase/sales agreement consistent with the oral agreement.[7] Of course, until the final purchase/sales agreement is signed by all parties, any oral agreement will not be binding. Nevertheless, reaching agreement orally on significant terms (and having a purchase/sales agreement drawn up accordingly thereafter) can sometimes cut down on the wasted "back and forth," and potentially, the expenses of having attorneys, realtors, or others revise, draw up, or redraw purchase/sales agreements.

In almost all real estate transactions, contingencies should be added to the standard purchase/sales agreement form. What is a contingency? A contingency is a matter written into a contract that, if a certain matter doesn't occur, allows a particular party to the contract to cancel the contract. Having a contingency in the purchase/sales agreement allows the benefiting party to "lock in" the other party but still permits the benefiting party an "out" if an important matter covered by the contingency is not met. Some common contingencies for a purchase/sales agreement for waterfront property include, but are not limited to, the following:

- Certain financing being available to the buyer at or before closing (for example, the ability to obtain a 30-year mortgage with 20% down and an interest rate of 6% or lower).
- The results of a property inspection being acceptable to the buyer.
- Positive test results for an on-site private septic system and water well.
- The occurrence of certain zoning and other municipal approvals.
- The buyer's (or his/her attorney's) approval of the title insurance commitment results and seller's title.
- The buyer's (or his/her attorney's) approval of survey results.

- The ability of the buyer to obtain a certain type of permit from the local government or from county or state officials, departments, or agencies before closing.

- A third-party appraisal valuing the property at a certain level or higher for financing or other purposes.

- Confirmation that the property is riparian and how much lake frontage is involved.

- The buyer's approval of environmental tests, inspections or reports (typically limited to non-residential properties).

Most contingencies benefit one party or the other, but rarely both the buyer and the seller.

In Michigan, if a property sale involves an existing dwelling, the seller must fill out a seller's disclosure statement pursuant to the Michigan Seller Disclosure Act, MCL 565.951 *et seq.*, and provide it to the prospective purchaser.[8] That form can be found in Attachment E. The disclosure statement should be delivered to the prospective buyer at or prior to the time that the purchase/sales agreement is signed. The disclosure statement can be delivered to the buyer at a later date, but it is important to note that the Seller Disclosure Act provides that the buyer may terminate the purchase/sales agreement within 72 hours after the disclosure form is personally delivered by the seller to the buyer (or within 120 hours if the disclosure statement is delivered by registered mail) if delivered after the purchase/sales contract is signed. Accordingly, a failure to deliver the disclosure statement when the contract is signed can provide a pitfall for a seller who believed that he/she had a binding agreement for the sale of the property.[9]

What happens if a contingency in a purchase/sales agreement is not met? Contingencies can run in favor of the purchaser, seller, or both. If a contingency is not met and the party benefited by the contingency properly notifies the other party in a timely fashion, the purchase/sales agreement is typically canceled, with no further obligation by either party (except for the normal obligation of the seller to return the buyer's earnest money to him/her).[10] One word of caution regarding contingencies involves proper notification from the party benefited by the contingency to the other party. Even if a contingency is not met, the benefiting party cannot benefit from that contingency's failure and cancel the agreement unless the benefiting party provides appropriate written notice (usually, as specified in the agreement) to the other party by some date specified in the agreement or prior to closing. If the notice requirements for "exercising" a contingency are not followed, the party otherwise benefited by the contingency may be deemed to have waived the right to cancel under that contingency and may be stuck with going through with the real estate transaction.

It is important to remember that canceling a purchase/sales agreement due to the failure of a contingency (which is lawful and consistent with the agreement) is different than breaching or breaking the agreement (which, of course, constitutes a breach of contract).

If both parties agree to a change, amendment, or modification of one or more terms of the purchase/sales agreement, it can be effectuated by a document signed by both parties, which is often referred to as an "addendum" to the purchase/sales agreement (although on occasion, it is called an "amendment").

What if one party to a purchase/sales agreement breaches or violates a provision of the agreement? Assuming that the person in apparent violation of the agreement is not properly exercising a contingency, they will have breached the agreement and are subject to potential penalties. While there are certain remedies available pursuant to statute and common law in Michigan, in many cases, the remedies for a breach of a purchase/sales agreement can actually be modified by a provision in the agreement itself. Normally, however, if one party breaches the purchase/sales agreement, the other party is entitled to "specific performance" should litigation arise. Specific performance is simply a court order requiring the breaching party to fulfill the terms of the agreement (usually, that means proceeding to a closing regarding the real estate involved). In some cases, if a prospective purchaser breaches a purchase/sales agreement and a closing cannot occur, the breaching purchasing party would likely forfeit their earnest money, but may also be subject to other additional penalties. On occasion, the "wronged party" can also recover damages from the breaching party.[11]

It should be kept in mind that a purchase/sales agreement does not, in and of itself, transfer title to real estate. Rather, it is a contract by which the parties agree to proceed to an eventual closing whereby title is formally transferred to the purchaser via a deed (or land contract) at closing if certain conditions and requirements are met. Accordingly, purchase/sales agreements normally are not recorded with the local county register of deeds.

On rare occasions, the parties may execute a short document entitled "Memorandum of Agreement" (or the equivalent) that is recorded with the county register of deeds to indicate to the public that a purchase/sales agreement has been entered into by the parties regarding a particular piece of property (*i.e.*, a sale is pending) and that a closing might occur regarding the property. That will give formal notice to the public, so that creditors and other potential buyers will have "record notice" of the pending potential sale.

What about "oral" purchase/sales agreements? In Michigan, oral contracts or agreements that do not involve real property or land are often enforceable. That is not the case with regard to purchase or sales agreements involving land in Michigan. Pursuant to the Michigan Statute of Frauds for the conveyance of interests in land (MCL 556.106, 556.108, and 556.132), all contracts regarding land must be in writing to be enforced. Furthermore, contracts for the sale of land in Michigan must meet certain minimum requirements in order to be enforceable. These are: the names of the parties involved, a description of the property involved, the sales price, and the performance (or closing) date. These requirements are sometimes referred to (and easily remembered) as the four "Ps" (*i.e.*, parties, property, price, and performance date).

By the way, contrary to popular myth, one cannot get out of a signed purchase/sales agreement due to the "fine print" based on a claim that the person did not understand the terms of the agreement. The general binding nature on both parties of a signed purchase/sales agreement for real estate in Michigan cannot be overstated (assuming that the document is properly drafted and contains no "loopholes").

Footnotes

[7] Some real estate professionals strongly disagree with this assessment and believe that the party who submits the first purchase/sales agreement (with their own wording) has a tactical advantage.

[8] Likewise, if a dwelling has lead paint (or was built prior to 1978), a similar disclosure must be made.

[9] A prospective purchaser should coordinate the seller disclosure statement with the purchaser's professional inspector.

[10] Many contingencies have an express time limit associated with them. Not acting within the time period can result in a sanction against the party otherwise benefiting from the contingency (for example, waiver of a right for inspection or cancellation based on inspection results, having to go through with the closing regardless, etc.).

[11] Sometimes, such damages can also include having to pay the commission or fee of one or more realtors or real estate agents.

Chapter 9
THE TIME PERIOD BETWEEN THE SIGNING OF THE PURCHASE/ SALES AGREEMENT AND CLOSING

THE TIME PERIOD BETWEEN THE EXECUTION OF THE purchase/sales agreement by both parties and the closing is extremely important. The due diligence attributable to this time should be pursued vigorously. This is the time period for the buyer in particular to do his/her homework!

The time period for closing should be specified in the purchase/sales agreement. There is no universally accepted time limit between the date on which a purchase/sales agreement is signed and when the closing actually occurs; however, rarely is that time period less than 20-30 days. Most closings occur within 30-90 days. Sometimes, the time period between the signing of the purchase/sales agreement and closing can be even longer than 90 days if one or more contingencies in the purchase/sales agreement will take a substantial period of time to satisfy, pursue, or eliminate. Buyers often prefer longer time periods, sellers shorter ones.

This is the time period during which the purchaser will pursue numerous contingencies, such as securing "firm" mortgage financing, having the dwelling or property inspections done, having his/her attorney review the title insurance commitment, and similar undertakings.

This is also the time period when a buyer (and preferably, the buyer's attorney) will review the title insurance commitment provided by the seller to make sure that title to the property is appropriate and that there are no liens, encumbrances, or other matters that would be problematic after closing.

The seller oftentimes is also busy during the preclosing time period doing such things as repairing items identified in the purchase/sales agreement, helping the buyer satisfy contingencies, and obtaining discharges of existing mortgage debt or other liens on the property.

Chapter 10
"CONTINGENCIES"

A "CONTINGENCY" IS AN ITEM OR CLAUSE PLACED in a purchase/sales agreement that allows either the prospective buyer or seller (or both) to back out of the deal prior to closing, generally without any penalty. While the overwhelming majority of contingencies are written in to protect the buyer, contingencies do sometimes benefit the seller.

Certain contingencies are typically contained within a form purchase/sales agreement contract, while others must be added. Sometimes, contingencies are contained in an "addendum," which is usually an attachment to the purchase/sales agreement at the time it is signed or added later pursuant to the agreement of the parties.

Some of the common contingencies in favor of a prospective buyer include the following:

- Being able to obtain mortgage or other financing to facilitate the purchase. Frequently, minimum requirements will be required for the financing, including the interest rate, loan time period, and similar matters.

- Buyer satisfaction with the title insurance commitment results and title of the seller.

- The ability of the property to support a private on-site septic system.
- The ability of the property to support a private well.
- An existing dwelling or other buildings being inspected by a professional home inspector and the results of such inspection being satisfactory to the buyer.
- The ability of the buyer to sell his/her existing residence.
- The ability of the buyer to obtain zoning and other municipal approvals for a new home or expansion or replacement of an existing dwelling.
- The ability of the seller to remove certain encumbrances, liens, or clouds on title before closing.
- The ability of the buyer to cancel the agreement if the results of specified environmental tests are not satisfactory to the buyer.
- The ability of a buyer to cancel a purchase/sales agreement if an appraisal does not meet a certain valuation number.
- Satisfaction by the buyer with survey results.
- A lack of negative uses (or the potential) nearby such as an airport, sewage plant, prison, expressway, landfill, power plant, mining operation, or industrial use.
- Verification that the property is not within a flood zone.
- Verification of the quality of the shoreline and depth of the water nearby.
- The ability to improve the shoreline (install a seawall, utilize shoreline landscaping, etc.)

Some of the contingencies frequently found in a purchase/sales agreement that favor the seller include the following:

- Seller satisfaction with a buyer's financing (or "pre-approval" to obtain financing).
- Seller's ability to purchase a specified replacement property.

In most cases, a contingency must be "exercised" or "waived" by a specified date. For example, most form residential purchase/sales agreements utilized by local real estate agents require that inspections be completed within 10 days after execution of the agreement. Buyers should be careful to ensure that they have enough time to conduct the necessary inspections, especially if the property is a second/vacation home and remotely located. Simply ignoring deadlines for contingencies is not a prudent course of action. If the beneficiary of a contingency does not properly assert the contingency, it is usually waived. In other words, nonaction usually results in waiver of a contingency. Furthermore, contingencies typically require a party to provide a written notice to the other party within a specified period of time. The notification requirements contained in a purchase/sales agreement should be followed precisely (for example, must such a notification be via email or must it be in a writing personally delivered, a writing sent by regular mail, or a writing sent by certified mail, return receipt requested?).

Chapter 11
INSPECTIONS AND INSPECTORS

AS A PART OF THE PROCESS OF BUYING ANY TYPE OF real property, it is normally prudent for a buyer to utilize one or more inspectors. That is particularly true of a waterfront property. It is also usually wise to "inspect" or investigate the area around the desired waterfront property.

If the waterfront property you are considering purchasing has a cottage, house, or other dwelling located thereon, you should definitely have a professional home inspector inspect the buildings and grounds before closing. This is one of those contingencies that must be written into the purchase/sales agreement, and the clause involved should allow the buyer to cancel the purchase/sales agreement (and receive the return of the earnest money) if the buyer is not satisfied with the results of the inspection and so notifies the seller in writing before closing. Make sure that you obtain the services of a fully qualified professional inspector, including an inspector who is bonded and has the appropriate insurance. While the overwhelming majority of professional home inspectors are highly skilled, there are some unqualified individuals out there who purport to be expert home inspectors but are not.[12] Termite inspections are also typically a "must."

If the waterfront property is vacant, are any inspections necessary? Typically, yes. For example, while some purchasers are content to rely on the results of a successful septic system permit or approval from the local health department, other buyers hire their own engineer or other professional to review the results of the health department tests and to also advise the buyer about what type of septic system will be needed, likely location(s), and the potential costs. In addition, local county health departments typically do not do testing for well locations, depth, or water quality before a well permit is issued. Depending upon the area and terrain, a prospective buyer might want to consult with an engineer or other professional regarding the likely suitability of the property for a private water well (and the cost of installing a well on the property).

"Buildability" generally means the ability of a property to have a new dwelling built on it, have an existing building be rebuilt, or have an addition added on to an existing building. Impediments to "buildability" on a particular property can be physical (for example, the presence of wetlands, proximity to a high-risk bluff, critical dune, or high-erosion area, the presence of a floodplain or flood zone, the inability to support an on-site septic system or well, or slopes too steep to build on) or legal (examples include deed restrictions that preclude any more dwellings or zoning regulations that make construction on-site expensive or even impossible). Inspectors or engineers can help with these issues.

If there are aspects of the property that will have to be altered to suit the needs of the prospective purchaser (such as leveling earth, the need for extensive fill, altering of wetlands, a new seawall, dredging, etc.), it will be very important for the prospective purchaser to hire the right inspector, engineer, or consultant to examine the land before closing. It may turn out that a prospective buyer will not be able to make those necessary modifications due to legal, topographical, cost, or other factors. In some cases, the prospective buyer may want to make the closing contingent upon the ability of such alterations to be made as evidenced by government permits to be obtained before closing. Again, if that is the case, the appropriate contingency language must be inserted into the purchase/sales agreement before it is signed by the parties.

It is often helpful to study a variety of maps of the area where the waterfront property is located, as well as charts and maps of the body of water itself. Such maps may show both desirable and undesirable traits of the area and body of water.

Inspections or investigations should not be limited solely to the lot or parcel involved. A prospective purchaser should investigate adjoining and nearby lots for negative matters. Also, the purchaser should be fully aware of any nearby uses that may negatively impact the waterfront lot being purchased (such as a nearby sewage plant, expressway, landfill, airport, prison, industrial use, or power plant).

Footnotes

[12] As of the date this book was written, Michigan did not require home inspectors to be formally licensed by the state. Accordingly, caution should be exercised when selecting a home inspector.

Chapter 12
SURVEYS

WHAT IS A SURVEY IN THE REAL PROPERTY (REAL estate) context? In common parlance, a survey is a written drawing made by a professional surveyor or engineer (licensed by the state of Michigan) that shows the location and placement of all boundary lines for a particular parcel or lot, as well as listing the property's legal description. Surveying work normally commences when a surveyor or engineer is provided the legal description for a particular property (often taken off the most recently recorded deed for the property). The surveyor or engineer then goes "into the field" (to the property) and uses various instruments, techniques, formulas, and calculations to "plot" the legal description on the earth. When the field work is done for most surveys, existing irons (monuments) are either found at the corners of the property, or, if the existing irons cannot be found or new parcels or lots are to be created, the surveying professional installs one or more new irons at the property corners. On occasion, at the request of the property owner or for other reasons, additional irons can be added at points other than the property corners for reference purposes. Typically, a surveying professional will also place a temporary wooden stake (often adorned with bright orange surveying tape) next to the corners where the irons are located, for easy reference by the property owner, financing bank, or other party. While the irons (typically, steel "rebar," that sticks an inch or two out of the ground) are meant to be permanent monuments, the wooden stakes are not permanent.[13] After the field work is done, the surveyor or engineer normally drafts a survey drawing to be given to the landowner, prospective purchaser, financing bank, or other party.

There are two general types of surveys. First, a conventional property survey is normally done to exacting specifications and is supposed to be extremely accurate. The second type of survey is frequently called a "mortgage survey" or "report" and is usually done to less exacting standards than a standard property survey. Typically, lending institutions (such as banks or credit unions) only require a mortgage survey before money is loaned regarding a property.

What does a typical survey drawing show? Common items draw on a survey map include:

- Boundary lines
- Buildings
- Easements
- Drives and sidewalks
- Encroachments
- Monuments
- Bodies of water
- Fences

What is a legal description? The legal description is the way that our society describes and locates property boundaries on the earth. Legal descriptions are created or generated (normally by a surveyor or engineer) when a parcel or lot is first created (*i.e.*, carved out of a larger piece of property). One cannot transfer title to a property by deed or land contract unless a property description has been generated for the lot or parcel involved and the description is placed in the deed or land contract.

Legal descriptions are generally of two types. First, an unplatted piece of property that is not a condominium unit is legally described by the "metes and bounds" technique. This system had its genesis in England before colonial days. It is a mathematical system. We have all seen this type of legal description— ... "thence S 3°43'55" W 127.73 feet; thence N 37°57'01" E 197.73 feet ..." Metes and bounds legal descriptions can be difficult to read and comprehend without formal training. The second type of legal description involves a platted lot or site condominium unit. These legal descriptions are easy to read. For example, one might buy title to "Lot 37 of the Acme Plat" or "Unit 5 of the Maple Valley Condominium."

Why are surveys done? In almost all instances, surveys are performed to ensure the accuracy of a legal description for a piece of property and to demonstrate "on the ground" where the boundary lines (or other items such as easements or public road rights-of-way) are located.

Who typically orders surveys and for what reasons? Persons and entities who commission surveys tend to fall into the following categories:

- A seller of real property.
- A prospective buyer of a property.
- A lending institution (bank, credit union, mortgage company, etc.) that is considering lending money for the purchase or improvement of a property.
- A landowner who wishes to verify the location of her property's boundary lines for purposes of determining whether the neighbor is encroaching, her house can be expanded, etc.
- Title companies.
- A governmental unit to determine right-of-way lines.
- A utility to locate utility easements.

Is a new survey really necessary when purchasing property? In almost all cases, **YES!!!** Why is a survey so important to a prospective purchaser of a property? There are many reasons. First, a survey will help ascertain whether the legal description that will ultimately be placed in the deed or land contract is accurate. Second, the survey (with the appropriate stakes and irons placed on-site) will show the prospective purchaser the physical limits of the property he is considering purchasing. It eliminates the guesswork as to where boundary lines are located and whether a purchaser is getting all of the land promised. Third, surveys will show and often highlight potential encroachments on, to, or from the property, including such things as the existence (and location) of an access easement encumbering the property, encroachment by the neighbor's garage onto the property, or the fact that the property really does not have frontage on the public road right of way. A survey can also often show whether a building, fence, or driveway on the property to be purchased encroaches on the neighbor's land. Fourth, it allows the title insurance company to remove certain exemptions from final title insurance policies in some cases. Fifth, a survey can identify potential defects in legal descriptions, boundary lines, and related matters. Sixth, for a waterfront property, a survey can confirm the amount of water frontage a parcel actually has. Finally, a survey can provide a purchaser with a higher level of comfort and assurance regarding many matters.

A buyer should require a <u>new</u> survey. Older surveys may not catch items of a more recent vintage such as a new encroachment or recently-granted easement.

Which party normally pays for a survey (performed after the purchase/sales agreement is signed but prior to closing), the seller or purchaser of the land involved? In Michigan, the typical practice is for the seller to pay for the survey at or prior to closing. Nevertheless, that is a cost item that can be negotiated between the parties and should be specified in the purchase/sales agreement.

One helpful, practical hint for any property owner who has had a survey done is to "cement in" the irons. That is, use a small trowel or shovel to dig down into the earth approximately three or four inches and around the iron for three or four inches outward without disturbing the iron. Then fill the "hole" around the iron with redi-mix cement, but leave an inch or two of the iron sticking up above the cement. Once the cement has hardened, you can put a little topsoil on top of the cement and plant it with grass seed. Irons have a way of being pulled out, damaged, or lost over time (thus necessitating a new survey), which this technique will generally prevent. Given that surveys can be costly, this helps ensure that the irons stay in place over the long run.

Footnotes

[13] Willfully removing, destroying, or defacing a survey monument (typically, an iron) is a misdemeanor in Michigan pursuant to MCL 54.210d. For plat monuments, see MCL 560.262. Such statutes are not applicable to the temporary wooden stakes placed adjacent to more permanent survey monuments.

Chapter 13
FINANCING AND EXPENSES

YOU MIGHT BE ONE OF THE RARE INDIVIDUALS WHO can pay cash for a Michigan lakefront property. Unfortunately, most purchasers of waterfront property must finance the purchase by borrowing.

There are generally two main ways in Michigan to finance a land transaction. The most common form of financing is to secure a long-term loan from a bank, credit union, or other financial institution. This is commonly referred to as a "mortgage." Technically, the actual mortgage is the document signed by the purchaser of the property in favor of the financing institution that is recorded with the county register of deeds. The written recorded mortgage evidences or "secures" the loan (it is a type of lien). The second most commonly used form of financing for real estate purchases in Michigan is a land contract. A land contract involves a long-term written agreement whereby the land purchaser makes monthly (or other periodic) payments to the seller over a long period of time. When all the required payments have been made (including interest), the seller gives a deed to the land purchaser for recording. Of course, both forms of land purchase financing involve the payment of interest.

Mortgages, land contracts, and the lending practices related to such financing are governed by a multitude of different state and federal statutes. Nevertheless, any potential borrower should satisfy himself or herself before entering into a finance agreement that he/she understands all the important aspects of the transaction. Should the land purchaser ultimately default on the mortgage or land contract (*i.e.*, breach the financing agreement by missing payments, laying waste to the property that secures the loan, etc.), the purchaser risks losing all interest in and title to the property involved.

If a prospective purchaser intends to finance the purchase of real property in Michigan through a bank or other lending institution loan secured by a mortgage, it is normally prudent to attempt to "prequalify" for such a loan beforehand. Essentially, that means meeting with an official of the bank or lending institution and having the financial institution do preliminary work regarding a potential loan to determine whether the borrowing party will eventually qualify for mortgage financing. A seller usually views a buyer's offer more favorably if the buyer includes a prequalification or preapproval letter from a bank regarding financing. That way, the seller knows that the buyer has the "wherewithal" to complete a closing. It makes no sense for a prospective purchaser to enter into a purchase/sales agreement for a piece of property only to be disappointed later prior to closing when he or she cannot secure mortgage financing. Furthermore, if the prospective purchaser does not ensure that the purchase/sales agreement contains an express contingency clause based on the ability to obtain mortgage financing and such financing cannot be obtained for closing, the prospective purchaser will be in breach of the purchase/sales agreement and could be forced to either go through with the purchase or potentially lose the earnest money and even be subject to additional financial penalties.

Following are some of the important issues that a prospective borrower should carefully review before entering into any type of agreement with a bank or financing institution for the mortgage financing of a purchase of real property or entering into a land contract:

- What is the true/effective interest rate?
- Is the interest rate variable or fixed?
- What is the term (length in months or years) of the mortgage or land contract?
- What are the penalties for late payments?

- Can the outstanding loan be "prepaid" (that is, paid off early without penalty)?

- What are the penalties for a default?

- Will the bank or seller "hold" the paper or potentially "sell" the loan to someone else so that you will be dealing with someone other than the original lending institution or seller of the property?

- If a mortgage loan, will you be paying "points"?

- What are the fees attendant to the mortgage to be paid at closing?

- If the property is sold, will the entire balance due on the mortgage be accelerated/due immediately ("due on sale" clause)?

A land contract is not available for most land purchasers, because sellers normally do not want to take the risk of financing the sale. Most sellers prefer "cash in hand" at closing. They want to "divorce" themselves from the property. Why, then, would a seller ever agree to sell a property on land contract? In most cases, a seller is only willing to sell a piece of property on land contract if the property is difficult to sell or has been on the market for some time. A major risk to a seller on a land contract is that the buyer will "trash" (*i.e.*, commit "waste" on) the dwelling or property involved, such that the property returned to the seller after a land contract default situation will be in poor condition when it reverts to the seller. Such risks make sellers reluctant to sell property on a land contract, even if the market interest rates on land contracts are quite high and attractive.

Land contracts can be advantageous to buyers. That is particularly true for higher risk buyers who are not able to obtain conventional financing from a bank or lending institution. However, there are two major drawbacks to land contracts for buyers. First, the interest rates tend to be higher than for conventional mortgage loans, as is the down payment. Second, buyers must normally wait many years before obtaining a deed to the property (when the land contract has been paid off in full). Sometimes, during the long term of the land contract, a seller can die or "sell" the seller's interest in the land contract to a third party (who might also sell the seller's land contract interest yet again to a subsequent party or parties). Finally, obtaining a deed when the land contract has been paid off can sometimes prove to be a challenge.[14]

If a buyer does not obtain a deed for the property until the land contract has been paid off, is the buyer really the "owner" of the property while the land contract is still pending? With a mortgage, the purchaser is truly the owner of the property involved (subject to a mortgage lien), but may lose his/her title to the property if he/she consistently defaults on payments under the mortgage. Yes, the purchaser under a land contract is, for all practical purposes, the "owner" of the property even while the land contract is pending. The buyer has the right to possession, control, etc., while the seller does not. The recording of the land contract (or a memorandum of land contract) with the county register of deeds tells the public that the land contract purchaser "owns" the real property at issue.

Although it used to be easier for a seller on a land contract to reclaim full title to (and possession of) the property involved if the buyer defaulted than was the case with a bank under a mortgage, that is no longer true under Michigan law. The degree of difficulty of reclaiming title to a property where a buyer has defaulted is roughly the same in Michigan for either a seller on a land contract or a bank via a mortgage.

When a land contract is paid off, the seller gives the buyer a deed to record with the county register of deeds. When a mortgage is paid off, how is it "cleared" from title so that the landowner will have unencumbered title to the property thereafter? Under Michigan law, the bank, financial institution, or other party that "holds the paper" regarding a mortgage must record a mortgage release with the county register of deeds where the mortgage was originally recorded within a certain period of time after the mortgage has been paid off.

When a prospective purchaser has entered into a purchase/sales agreement for a piece of property, that person will want to make sure on the title insurance commitment (issued before closing) that there are no outstanding mortgages or land contracts on the property involved or that they will be fully discharged as of record at or prior to the closing. A purchaser of real estate certainly does not want to buy property that will still be subject to an old or prior mortgage or land contract for which the new buyer will still be responsible!

As with many real estate closing documents, mortgages and land contracts tend to be long, complicated documents. If in doubt, have your real estate attorney review the documents in detail before closing.

In Michigan, there are limits on the maximum interest rates that can be charged by lenders pursuant to a land contract or mortgage financing. If an interest rate is charged in excess of the legal limit, the interest rate is deemed to be "usurious" and no interest at all can be collected under law if the borrower successfully challenges the interest rate in court.

Footnotes

[14] This can be remedied by having the seller sign a deed at closing that is held in escrow by a third party until the land contract is paid off. The deed is then recorded.

Chapter 14
"TALK TO OTHERS ..."

ONE OF THE BEST OPTIONS AVAILABLE TO prospective purchasers of a waterfront property is conversation. It is normally prudent for a prospective purchaser of a waterfront property to contact officials of the local municipality (often, the zoning administrator, tax assessor, or municipal clerk) and quiz them about the characteristics of the lake involved, as well as ask them whether they are familiar with any problems associated with the particular lot or parcel at issue. Local municipal officials can be a wealth of information and are normally more than happy to discuss such matters (as well as zoning, buildability, and other issues) with a prospective purchaser.

It is also frequently helpful to talk to the neighboring riparian landowners before purchasing the parcel or lot at issue. It is normally prudent to also contact one of the officers of the lake or river property owners association (if one exists), and question them regarding the characteristics of the water body involved, problems that have arisen, whether they are familiar with the lot or parcel at issue, and related matters. If a prospective purchaser really wants to be diligent, he or she should attempt to track down the person(s) who owned the parcel or lot at issue prior to the current owner. Frequently, that can be done by getting copies of past deeds or obtaining past property tax records from the local municipality. Of course, if the property you are considering was the home mailing address for such past owners, their current address will not show up on such deed or tax record; but sometimes they can still be located. Frequently, past owners of a lakefront property are only too happy to discuss the "pros" and "cons" of their former property with a prospective purchaser. It can also be useful to talk to the owner of a nearby bait and tackle shop, a county marine patrol officer, or the local game warden about the lake or portion of the lake in which you are interested.

Finally, it is often helpful to talk to (or even retain) a realtor or real estate agent or broker who specializes in the type of waterfront property at interest in the geographical area desired.

Chapter 15
ENCUMBRANCES

WHAT IS AN ENCUMBRANCE?[15] **IT IS A LEGAL TERM** for anything that affects or limits the title of a piece of real estate, such as a mortgage, easement, lien, lease, judgment, deed restriction, or similar item. It is a legal "burden" on the property, which takes away or detracts from the property owner's title. Most encumbrances are a claim by or liability to a third party that attaches to the real property of another. Most (but not all) encumbrances on real property are "liens." A lien is a legal claim on or a security interest in the real property of another. Generally, a lien secures (or is collateral for) a debt or other obligation. Typically, the beneficiary of a lien on a property is a "creditor."

The following are some of the miscellaneous types of liens and encumbrances:

- Property tax liens.
- Special assessment district liens.
- Construction liens (formerly, mechanics liens).
- Attorney fees liens.
- Court orders or judgments (monetary) — these can include divorce judgments, monetary judgments secured by the land, etc.

- Court judgments or orders for property violations of state statutes or local ordinances.
- State (non-property tax) tax liens.
- Federal (IRS) tax liens.
- Mortgages.
- Environmental liens.
- Land contract seller's interest.
- Land contract buyer's interest.
- Deed restrictions/restrictive covenants.
- Dower interest of a wife.
- A lease.
- Memorandum of purchase agreement (the seller is trying to sell the property to someone else).
- A memorandum for some other type of unrecorded agreement.
- A notice lis pendens (meaning there is pending litigation regarding the property).
- An affidavit regarding the property.
- Notice of an adverse possession, prescriptive easement, or acquiescence claim.
- A severance of mineral rights or a mineral lease (can be gas, oil, sand, gravel, etc.).
- Notice of delinquent dues, annual assessment, etc. (typically, with a condominium association or a lake association with deed restrictions).
- An easement or right-of-way.
- A license.

Does it really matter if the purchaser of a waterfront property owns the mineral rights to that land? Some purchasers of real estate in Michigan do not always obtain the mineral rights to the property or obtain those rights free and clear (for example, the mineral rights might have been sold to someone else or be subject to a recorded oil and gas or other lease). In Michigan, mineral rights can be "detached" or severed from the ownership of the surface of the land and can be transferred or leased separately from the land's surface. Therefore, if you purchase a waterfront property in

Michigan, it is possible that you will not obtain the mineral rights or, even if you do, they may be subject to a long-term oil and gas or other lease over which you have no control and for which you will receive no compensation.

Some people believe it really does not matter whether a waterfront property owner has control over the mineral rights for that land. The theory is that since the environmental laws will not allow an oil and gas rig to be installed near a body of water, the likelihood of severed mineral rights being a problem in the future is unlikely for a waterfront property owner. However, there are at least two errors in that logic. First, while oil and gas rigs cannot be installed close to a body of water in Michigan, property owners who have their mineral rights can often financially benefit from oil and gas activity, even where their property is located a mile away from any rig. How is that possible? In Michigan, oil and gas leases or rights are typically bundled together or "pooled," so that an oil and gas company controls all mineral rights for a square mile or even larger area. Typically, an oil and gas rig "pulls" oil or gas underground from a fairly large area, thus necessitating tying up all the mineral rights for a significant geographical area. Accordingly, even the owners of small waterfront properties can potentially obtain lucrative oil and gas royalties for a new drilling operation that might be located half a mile away from their property or even farther. If someone purchases a waterfront property without the mineral rights or subject to an oil and gas lease, they will not participate in any profits from such a pooling arrangement.

The second problem associated with not obtaining control of mineral rights pursuant to the purchase of a waterfront property involves large waterfront properties. Sand and gravel are also minerals, and extensive sand and gravel mining operations can occur fairly close to Michigan lakes and streams. Furthermore, if one purchases a large acreage waterfront property, the possibility of having an oil or gas well on or near the property increases the farther away from the river or lake the property extends.

Footnotes

[15] An "encumbrance" should not be confused with an "encroachment." The former is a legal term for something affecting title to real property. The latter is a physical intrusion into or onto the property of another. See Chapter 17.

Chapter 16
DEED RESTRICTIONS, CONDOMINIUM ASSOCIATIONS, AND MANDATORY PROPERTY OWNERS ASSOCIATIONS

MOST WATERFRONT PROPERTIES IN MICHIGAN ARE not subject to deed restrictions and are not within a condominium development, such that the owner of the waterfront property is not obligated to belong to a lake, condominium, or other property owners association. Nevertheless, there are enough waterfront properties in Michigan that fall into one or more of those categories that a prospective purchaser of a waterfront property should look closely into these matters before signing a purchase/sales agreement.

A significant number of waterfront properties in Michigan are bound by deed restrictions (also sometimes referred to as a restrictive covenant or covenants). A deed restriction is a rule or regulation (generally permanent) that binds one property, several properties, or many properties. In most cases, they are permanent and "run with the land" (which means that they bind the current and all future owners of the property). Normally, deed restrictions are a positive characteristic of a property, development, or neighborhood; that is, deed restrictions tend to prohibit negative matters and enhance the values of the properties involved. For example, typical deed restrictions can include prohibitions against mobile homes, nuisances, businesses within residential areas, the further splitting or dividing of lots or parcels, the outdoor storage of junk, and other undesirable items, uses, or activities. Deed restrictions can also require affirmative obligations of the property owners such as the payment of annual dues to support a property owners association, keeping the exterior of every dwelling in good repair, requiring that all new construction be approved by a committee based on architecture, and contributing to the joint maintenance of a common private road or park.

Deed restrictions are mandatory. If a property owner violates one of the deed restrictions, the property owner's neighbors or a property owners association can go to court if necessary to enforce the deed restriction. If you purchase a property that is subject to a deed restriction or restrictions, plan on being bound by the regulations contained in the covenant(s) comprising the deed restriction(s). A prospective land purchaser should carefully review any restrictions that show up in the title insurance commitment and exercise any related contingency to cancel the closing if the purchaser cannot live with the restriction(s). Deed restrictions can have a dramatic impact upon property values, both positive and negative.

A few waterfront properties in Michigan are located within a summer resort association created via one of Michigan's ancient summer resort statutes. Those statutes are as follows:

- The Summer Resort and Park Associations Act of 1897 (MCL 455.1 *et seq.*)

- The Summer Resort and Assembly Associations Act of 1889 (MCL 455.51 *et seq.*)

- The Suburban Homestead, Villa-Park and Summer Resort Associations Act of 1887 (MCL 455.101).

- The Summer Resort Owners Act of 1929 (MCL 455.201 *et seq.*)

Prospective purchasers of a property in one of Michigan's statutory summer resorts must exercise extreme caution. In many cases, the purchaser of such a property might not actually obtain a deed or land contract for a lot or parcel, but rather a mere stock certificate or right of usage. Furthermore, such summer resort associations are typically subject to very strict rules and regulations (akin to deed restrictions/restrictive covenants) and may have other characteristics with which some purchasers might not feel comfortable. For more information regarding Michigan's summer resort associations, please see Chapter 10 of the Michigan Lake & Stream Associations, Inc. book entitled *Michigan Lake Associations – The Nuts and Bolts*. (Please see Attachment L for an order form for that book.)

Chapter 17
ENCROACHMENTS AND "SQUATTER'S RIGHTS"

IN REAL PROPERTY TERMINOLOGY, WHAT IS AN "encroachment"? An encroachment is when an item belonging to one property (such as a driveway, house, accessory building, fence, sidewalk, or similar item) spills over the common lot line onto the property of another. In some cases, the encroachment is known to the owners of both properties, while in other cases, encroachments do not come to light until a survey has been done of one or both properties. Possible encroachments are one of the reasons why a prospective purchaser of a lakefront property should insist on a new survey being done (and the results thereof being satisfactory to the buyer) before closing.

Encroachments can be a potential problem to both the seller and buyer of a property with an encroachment or that causes an encroachment on an adjoining property of a third party. Encroachments, whether on the property to be purchased or caused by the property to be purchased, mean purchasing a potential headache. If the encroachment is on the property being purchased, the adjoining property owner may be able to claim that portion of property by adverse possession or obtain a permanent encroachment right via a prescriptive easement. Should that occur, the purchaser will not only have a "cloud" on title on the property being purchased, but the buyer might potentially lose that portion of the property. If the property to be purchased has an encroachment on the adjoining property of a third party, the buyer might have to spend money removing the encroachment (for example, moving the driveway entirely back onto the property being purchased, moving an accessory building, etc.).

For a seller of property involving an encroachment, problems that might arise are the reverse situation of a prospective purchaser. Encroachments either on the property involved or caused by the property involved can make selling the property a difficult proposition for the seller. Encroachments that only show up at the last minute before closing can either lead the buyer to cancel the purchase/sales agreement or result in a significantly delayed closing while the encroachment is being remedied. If an encroachment on the property being purchased is not discovered until after closing and the seller gave a warranty deed to the buyer, the seller could be on the hook for resolving the encroachment out of the seller's pocket. If an encroachment is not resolved, it can result in an adverse possession or a prescriptive easement claim.

Nearly every riparian property owner has heard the phrases squatter's rights, adverse possession, and prescriptive easement. But what do they mean? There seems to be a great deal of confusion out there regarding these concepts. In general, if you use the land of an adjoining or nearby property owner in a certain fashion for in excess of 15 years, under certain circumstances, you can claim title to that portion of land or an easement over it. The phrase "squatter's rights" is a common vernacular for the legal doctrine of "adverse possession." Adverse possession is a process whereby one property owner can potentially claim actual title to certain adjoining property.

In order for someone to successfully claim title via adverse possession to property which was not previously theirs, two things must occur. First, the person must have used the adjoining property of another for 15 years or more in a fashion which was open and notorious (*i.e.*, in a way which was regular and highly visible), exclusive (it cannot have also been used concurrently during that 15 years by the true owner of the property), hostile (not meaning nasty or mean, but without the permission of the true landowner) and under claim of right (you were treating the property as your own and you are an adjoining property owner). Second, someone claiming property through adverse possession cannot actually obtain true title to the property until a successful court action awards such title.

A prescriptive easement is similar to adverse possession, but instead of obtaining exclusive title to a strip of land, one merely obtains a permanent easement for a particular use. For example, suppose a neighbor utilizes a driveway across your property for in excess of 15 years without your permission. Or alternately, the owner of a non-lakefront lot across the road uses a path down to the lake across your waterfront property and maintains a dock on your lakefront at the end of that path for over 15 years. Under certain circumstances, your neighbor could obtain a permanent prescriptive easement for such uses in court if the neighbor proves the same general elements which are required for adverse possession (*i.e.*, lack of permission, open use for over 15 years, etc.) but not requiring exclusive use.

Prescriptive rights can also sometimes be utilized by someone to expand existing easement usage rights. For example, assume that a backlot owner has an express easement to utilize a riparian property for access purposes only to a lake—the original easement rights did not include the right to dockage, permanent boat moorage, sunbathing, etc. If the beneficiary of that easement utilizes the easement for sunbathing, one dock and one boat for over 15 years without the permission of the underlying property owner, the backlot owner might gain the right to continue those activities permanently pursuant to court action under the theory of expanded rights by prescriptive easement.

Adverse possession and prescriptive easement controversies tend to arise more frequently with regard to lake property than other property. Why? Probably because many lake lots are small, were created many years ago, and have seemingly overlapping boundary lines. Given that many riparian lots are small and increasingly valuable, every inch of waterfront property is important. Battles involving alleged prescriptive easement rights to lakes are also increasing around the state. The owners of back lots are using this legal doctrine to access lakes where no express easement exists or to expand the usage rights for recorded lake access easements that were originally for access purposes only. Finally, for whatever reason, many people tend to be more emotional and territorial regarding waterfront property boundaries than for most other lands.

Contrary to popular myth, it is not easy to obtain title to a piece of land by adverse possession or an easement via prescriptive easement. Nevertheless, property owners should be on guard if it appears that other landowners in the area are attempting to use property in such a way as to commence the 15-year adverse possession or prescriptive easement time clock. That claim can be broken prior to the running of the 15-year time limit by either stopping the adverse use of the property, granting express permission for such use (which will remove the "hostility" requirement), or filing an ejectment lawsuit.

Incredible as it may seem, someone who gains title to a piece of land by adverse possession or a permanent prescriptive easement normally does not have to pay the former owner of the land for the property or lakefront obtained!

Since this is a relatively complex area of real estate law, you should consult with your own attorney immediately if you believe someone is attempting to accrue an adverse possession or prescriptive easement right to your property. This is certainly one area where it is not wise to "let sleeping dogs lie," since delay could permit someone to pass the 15-year time hurdle.

Chapter 18
THE CLOSING

THE CLOSING IS THE CLIMAX OF A REAL ESTATE purchase transaction. All the preparation work comes together at or prior to closing. At closing, the buyer and seller generally meet in person (although a few closings do occur where the parties sign the documents at the title insurance company office separately and at different times), the seller is paid the purchase price, and the buyer obtains a deed or land contract for the property. A "closing checklist" can be found at Attachment F.

Today, most closings occur at a branch office of the title insurance company or agent that handles the title insurance for the transaction. It is typically the title insurance company that drafts all of the closing documents for most waterfront property purchase closings. Title insurance companies will normally handle such documents and provide a location to close (as well as a title insurance company employee to assist) for a relatively modest fee or fees in addition to the premium for the title insurance policy itself.

Typical documents that must be signed at closing include the following:

- A deed or land contract by the seller.
- A seller's closing statement (sometimes called a "seller's settlement statement").

- A buyer's closing statement (sometimes called a "buyer's settlement statement").

- A buyer's mortgage and promissory note, if applicable, together with other loan-related documents.

- An "owner's affidavit" signed by the seller certifying that no recordable events have occurred since the date that the title commitment was issued and that no unrecorded facts or circumstances exist which may result in a claim against the property or the issued title insurance policy (such as unrecorded construction liens, seller bankruptcy filings, etc.).

- Michigan property transfer affidavit (notifying the local municipal property tax assessor of the change in ownership and the name and address of the new taxpayer).

- Michigan homestead tax exemption documents (where the purchased dwelling will be the buyer's primary residence).

- Waiver documents indicating that the title insurance company has not rendered legal advice and is not responsible for certain matters.

- Miscellaneous disclosure form(s).

- Tax documents (such as a substitute 1099 IRS form).

- Removal or satisfaction of contingencies document.

- Bill of sale (where applicable).

- Miscellaneous forms.

The buyer will have to provide certified funds at closing (such as a certified or cashier's check). Personal checks are normally not accepted by the title insurance company. In addition, it is not uncommon for the title insurance company to require that the certified or cashier's check be made out to the title insurance company, rather than the seller, as the title insurance company will disburse funds by issuing separate checks for whatever funds and costs are allocated to the buyer, seller, register of deeds, local property taxing authority, etc.

Normally, it is prudent for each party (or each party's attorney) to request that the title insurance company provide to him or her copies of all closing documents at least several days before closing. That will give each party (or the party's attorney) sufficient time to review the documents in detail and to request any corrections prior to closing. Given the somewhat large number of documents usually involved at closing, it is normally not prudent to wait to review them for the first time at the closing.

If a closing occurs at a title insurance company office, that firm will be responsible for most of the follow-up regarding the closing documents. The title insurance company will record the signed deed or land contract (or a memorandum of land contract), along with any discharge of a mortgage, with the county register of deeds. Any federal or state tax documents that are executed at closing will be forwarded by the insurance company to the appropriate governmental units. The funds will normally be disbursed at closing. Typically, the buyer will receive the original deed or land contract back from the register of deeds office via the mail (after it has been "stamped" and recorded with the county register of deeds) several weeks after closing. The buyer should receive the original of the title insurance policy within one or two months of closing, and if not, the buyer should contact the title insurance company to make sure that the original policy arrives.

Given some of the financing problems that arose nationally in the recent past, title insurance companies typically require both the buyer and seller to present proof of who they are by producing their driver's licenses at closing. Some title insurance companies also require the buyer and seller to sign affidavits of identity or the equivalent at closing.

In almost all circumstances, any and all contingencies contained in a purchase/sales agreement must be satisfied at or prior to closing. If a contingency has not been satisfied and the closing occurs and is completed, in most cases, the contingency is deemed waived by the otherwise benefiting party.

Both the buyer and seller should keep any originals and copies of all documents signed at closing permanently and in a safe place. It is sometimes necessary to be able to reconstruct events leading up to and at the closing regarding a real estate transaction later, often years in the future. While a title insurance company office (or even the real estate broker, agent, or realtor) may keep extra copies of all signed closing documents for some period of time, there is no guarantee that those copies will be available from the title insurance company should the buyer or seller need them years later.

Of course, there are some real estate transactions regarding waterfront properties whereby the standard closing documents will have to be supplemented by custom documents or forms drafted by the parties or their attorneys. In some instances, it is necessary to have one's attorney be present at a closing, while in other cases, it is sufficient to have the attorney review all of the documents beforehand (with no necessity that the attorney be physically present at closing). Sometimes, closings will occur at places other than a title insurance company, such as a realtor or attorney's office. While that can be convenient for the parties, it is sometimes helpful to have the closing occur on the "neutral" territory provided by the title insurance company's offices. Wherever the closing is held, it is always important to have access to a copy machine so that everyone can leave closing with a complete copy of all of the signed, if yet unrecorded, documents.

There is a little trick that a purchaser of real estate can do at closing to make sure that no last-minute liens or other encumbrances have attached to the title of the property that were not covered by the title insurance commitment. Remember, the title insurance commitment is issued weeks or even months before closing. The title insurance commitment is based upon a search of the public record for the property at a particular point in time to determine documents that were recorded with the register of deeds. The title commitment guarantees that the title insurance company will issue a title insurance policy after closing consistent with the title insurance commitment. If, between the time the title insurance commitment is issued and closing, an additional lien or other encumbrance in a document is recorded with the county register of deeds, neither the title insurance company nor the parties will know about it at closing and the title insurance policy may not insure against that new lien or encumbrance. While some title insurance companies update their title commitments as of the day of closing, not all do so. Therefore, it is normally prudent for the purchaser of real property to ask the title insurance company to update the title insurance commitment up to the date and time of closing, which can be formally notated by having the title insurance company agent date, initial, and write down the date and time of the update on the buyer's copy of the title insurance commitment at closing.

Chapter 19
WHO PAYS
FOR WHAT
AT CLOSING?

APART FROM THE PURCHASE PRICE, THE PARTIES TO
a real estate closing can theoretically negotiate (and specify in
the purchase/sales agreement) which party pays for what costs
and expenses of closing. Typical closing costs include costs and
expenses associated with title insurance, document preparation,
recording fees, real estate transfer taxes, proration (reimbursement)
of real property taxes, and similar matters. In some regions of
Michigan, "local practice" tends to allocate certain closing costs
to particular parties. Nevertheless, those costs can always be
specifically allocated however the parties themselves desire
pursuant to the purchase/sales agreement. One example of local
practice involves the proration of real property taxes. Although a
statute exists which provides a mechanism for the apportionment
of property taxes, by custom, the apportionment/proration
typically works as follows (unless modified by the purchase/sales
agreement).

The seller pays for all real property taxes and installments of
special assessments first billed in the years prior to the year in
which closing occurs. The buyer pays for all real property taxes and
installments of special assessments first billed in the years after the
year in which the closing occurs. Real property taxes and special
assessments first billed in the year in which closing occurs are

usually "prorated" between the parties by adding the amount of the December and July tax bills for the year in which closing occurs and dividing by 365 to establish a per-diem (per day) rate. (Where the tax bills for the current year are not yet available, the prior year's bills are used, sometimes with a multiplier such as "103% of the prior year" to account for inflation.) The per-diem rate is then multiplied by the number of days in the year up to the closing date to determine the seller's responsibility for the taxes due in the year of closing, with the buyer paying the difference. Complicated? Often, yes. A buyer will frequently have to rely on their own realtor, real estate broker, real estate agent, attorney, or the closing title insurance office to ensure that prorations are correct.

A savvy seller may find that specifying that each party will pay for taxes billed during his/her tenure of ownership (*i.e.,* no proration) is beneficial if the closing occurs early in the year, because it may allow ownership of the property for a portion of the year without payment of any taxes. On the other hand, if the seller would be required to pay the summer tax bill, which in most cases is the bulk of the taxes due for the year, shortly before closing, then proration on a calendar year basis would usually be more beneficial to the seller.

Chapter 20
TITLE INSURANCE

IN THE "OLD DAYS," THERE WAS NO TITLE INSURANCE for purchasers of real property in Michigan. Rather, real estate buyers (or their attorneys) reviewed abstracts or attorney opinions regarding title. An abstract was generally just a listing of all prior recorded documents regarding the property involved going back a certain number of years. Abstracts told lay people very little. A lawyer's opinion dealt with whether or not the seller had proper title and any limitations upon that title. Neither the old abstracts nor attorney title opinions were insurance as such, and they really did not constitute reliable guarantees of proper title to the purchaser.

Insurance companies eventually introduced a product often referred to as "title insurance." Title insurance is very important for almost all real property purchases, but particularly so where a waterfront property is involved. The issuance of title insurance is a two-step process. Almost all purchase/sales agreements call on the seller to provide to the buyer a "title insurance commitment" before closing and a title insurance policy after closing. Typically, both are issued in an amount equal to the purchase price. A title insurance commitment is usually issued by a title insurance company before closing and allows the prospective purchaser (and potentially, his or her attorney) to see whether the seller has good title, whether there are any encumbrances on the property, what the property taxes are annually, any requirements for closing, and similar matters. See the Attachment G sample. Before issuing a title insurance commitment, the title company does a title search of the property, looking for relevant documents recorded with the local county register of deeds regarding the property. Once a title insurance commitment is issued, the title company is affirming that it will issue a final title insurance policy in favor of the buyer after closing with all of the requirements, exceptions, and limitations contained in the title insurance commitment. Typically, the seller pays for both the title insurance commitment and the eventual title insurance (although there is generally one overall fee for both), unless the purchase/sales agreement provides otherwise.

Rarely does title insurance insure riparian rights, bottomlands, or similar matters unless the parties purchase a special rider or coverage (which may not even be available in many cases).

A formal final title insurance policy is usually issued (and sent) to the buyer a few months after the closing. The buyer should take great care to preserve the original of the title insurance policy forever. Furthermore, it is often prudent to make copies of the actual original title insurance policy and to store the copies at a different location than the actual original document (that is also true with the deed or land contract after closing and recording). Title insurance guarantees good title, lack of encumbrances, etc., apart from those items which are expressly "carved out" or exempted in the title insurance commitment and title insurance policy. Normally, the title insurance will cover attorney fees and costs for an attorney provided by the title insurance company to the buyer to defend the buyer's title as well as any damages that might be incurred by the purchaser of the real property caused by a matter covered by the title insurance policy.

It has also become very common for real estate closings in Michigan to occur at the offices of the title insurance company (or its agent or affiliate) and for the title insurance company to provide many of the closing documents (the deed or land contract, any mortgage, etc.) for an additional fee(s).

Chapter 21
THE DEED OR LAND CONTRACT

AT CLOSING, TITLE IS TRANSFERRED FROM THE SELLER to the buyer via either a deed or land contract. The seller (or sellers) signs the deed or land contract in front of a notary. The notary must also sign and "notarize" the document.[16] Ultimately, the executed deed or land contract (or memorandum of land contract) is recorded with the county register of deeds. If the closing occurs at a title insurance company, the title insurance company will typically record the finished document.

Why is a deed or land contract (or memorandum of land contract) recorded with the register of deeds for the county in which the land is located? To give the general public "record notice" of the document. Why is that important? There are several reasons. First, it helps prevent an unscrupulous seller from selling the same land twice to two different, unsuspecting buyers. Second, it gives record notice to everyone that the land has been sold (and to whom). Third, it alerts the local tax assessor that a real estate transfer has occurred. Fourth, it preserves the transaction, even if the recorded document is later lost or destroyed.

Many lay people are surprised at the lack of formality attending most deeds or land contracts. Remember, a deed or land contract is simply a document prepared by one of the parties (or the title insurance company) that is signed by the seller or sellers (or by all parties if a land contract). Michigan does not have a real property system whereby deeds or land contracts are issued or certified by the state of Michigan. This is not a transaction akin to a vehicle title transfer, with a state-issued new title document.

There are several different types of deeds. The most common type of deed is a warranty deed, whereby the seller makes certain warranties (or guarantees) regarding the title being transferred. See Attachment H. Of course, the warranty itself is only as good as the seller is solvent. However, if title insurance is issued to the buyer, that title insurance will typically back up the seller's warranty of title. Quitclaim deeds are less common in arm's-length real estate purchases. A quitclaim deed does not contain any warranty of title; that is, the seller simply indicates that whatever title he or she has in the property (if any) is being transferred to the buyer. See Attachment I. If the seller does not have any title or has inadequate title, the buyer will not obtain full title to the property. For example, it is perfectly legal for someone to issue a quitclaim deed for the Mackinaw Bridge to someone else. (Of course, if the "seller" misrepresents the transaction and "sells" the Mackinaw Bridge to the buyer for a sum of money, that could constitute criminal fraud.) Sometimes, judicial deeds, sheriff's deeds, or personal representative deeds are utilized. A personal representative deed is often used by the personal representative of a probate estate. The deed only warrants that the personal representative did nothing to cause a defect in title while acting as the personal representative. A sheriff's deed is typically used to convey title after a mortgage foreclosure or a property tax foreclosure sale.[17]

Land contracts are utilized to transfer title to real property in Michigan, but they are not as common as they used to be. A land contract is a formal contract or agreement entered into between a seller of real property and a buyer that extends for a number of years and provides that the buyer will obtain full title to the property involved via a later deed when the land contract ends and all payments pursuant to the land contract have been made. See Attachment J. During the time that the land contract is in effect, the seller retains formal record title to the property. When the land contract is finished and the land has been paid off, the seller then gives a deed to the buyer (and the deed is recorded). This transaction is similar to where a bank or other lending institution loans money to the purchaser of a property and utilizes a mortgage to secure the loan. The mortgage is discharged (removed) when the loan has been paid off. So, too, is a land contract a method of financing a property purchase. However, it is the seller who is financing the purchase for the buyer rather than a bank.

Land contracts tend to be rather lengthy, as the contract must specify all of the rights, duties, and other matters between the parties. In the past, it was slightly easier for a seller to regain possession of property pursuant to a land contract default than it was for a lender to foreclose on a mortgage. Today, the degree of difficulty of the seller or lender regaining possession and full title to the property financed is roughly the same for both a mortgage and a land contract.

The interest rate (and the amount of money a buyer has to put down at closing) tends to be higher for a land contract than for a bank mortgage loan. Sometimes, if credit is tight, a seller has little choice but to consider a land contract sale if he/she wants to sell the property expeditiously.

Land contracts are generally disfavored for sellers for a number of reasons. First, the seller does not receive all of the sale proceeds at once and is essentially financing the buyer's purchase of the property. Second, sellers sometimes get the property back when a buyer has defaulted on the land contract. It is also not uncommon for a buyer to "trash" the property (*i.e.,* commit "waste") before the seller regains possession of the property from the defaulting purchaser. Third, collecting payments over a number of years can be bothersome. And finally, although a seller will eventually have to give a deed when a land contract is paid off, that is not always that easy. Sometimes, the land contracting seller is a married couple where divorce occurs. Or, where there are multiple sellers, one or more of the sellers may have moved away and be hard to locate in order to sign a deed when a land contract has been paid off.[18]

Sometimes, parties to a real estate transaction do not wish to have members of the general public see all of the terms and conditions contained in a land contract, but want to record something with the county register of deeds for public notice purposes. In those cases, both parties can sign a memorandum of the land contract, which can be recorded with the county register of deeds in lieu of recording the land contract itself. A memorandum of land contract gives members of the public general notice that a sale of a particular property has occurred but does not contain all of the intimate details and conditions of the land contract itself.

Typically, deeds (and land contracts) must contain certain clauses or provisions. Such language can include, but is not always limited to, the following:

- The parties' names and addresses.
- The property's legal description.
- Title warranties (if any).
- The seller(s) signature(s).
- The notary block.
- Transfer tax language.
- "Drafted by" disclosure.
- Amount paid ("consideration").
- Land Division Act disclosures (near a farm, division rights transferred, etc.).
- Date.
- "Subject to" language.
- Restrictions (if any).

Footnotes

[16] In the past, a deed or land contract also had to be signed by two witnesses. That statutory requirement was deleted a number of years ago.

[17] Extreme caution should be exercised regarding a title based on a deed after a foreclosure or a tax sale. Title may be defective if the proper procedures were not utilized. Unfortunately, in the aftermath of the housing finance bubble collapse, prospective purchasers of foreclosed properties have frequently been unable to close on the purchase of such real estate due to the large number of foreclosure proceeding errors that have been made. When dealing with a real estate title derived from a foreclosure or tax sale, it is important to consult with legal counsel at an early stage and to also make certain that title insurance will cover and guarantee all title matters.

[18] Frequently, the seller or sellers sign a deed at the time the land contract is entered into and the deed is "held in escrow" by some third party to be delivered to the land contract purchaser once the land contract has been paid off.

Chapter 22
WHAT TYPE OF TITLE SHOULD BE OBTAINED?

PURCHASERS OF REAL PROPERTY CAN OBTAIN several different types of title to real estate. The types of title (or, put another way, the ownership rights obtained in real property) can be complete, such as fee simple absolute title (the best or most complete title), or non-complete, such as a life estate, a defeasible title, a lease, a license, or some other limited title.

Technically, a person does not own real estate in Michigan. Rather, a person owns an "estate" in land. An estate can be defined as "the amount, degree, nature, and quality of a person's interest in lands or other property." *Black's Law Dictionary 567* (7th Ed 1999). The "estate" concept—which goes back to old England—does not usually connote that one owns a large mansion and thousands of acres of land!

Fee simple or fee simple absolute title is the best title that one can obtain to a piece of real estate. Such title normally means that the owner of the property owns all major property interests and has "good and marketable title." Having "marketable title" means having clear title, or that there are no significant defects that would prevent the purchaser from freely selling, conveying, or mortgaging the real estate. Normally, when someone has fee simple absolute title, they are deemed to own the property forever, at least until the property is sold or transferred (or the person dies and title goes to a trust, probate estate, etc.)

Fee simple title is often analogized to a full bundle of sticks. Each stick in the bundle represents a partial property right. A person who holds fee simple or fee simple absolute title possesses the full bundle of sticks with none missing. If another person were to obtain an interest in the property (*i.e.,* through a recorded easement), one of the sticks would be removed from the bundle. That is, the easement would be "owned" by someone else, such that the owner of the property on which the easement is located would no longer "own" the whole bundle of sticks.

In Michigan, there are also estates or title of limited duration which would not represent a full bundle of sticks. Extreme caution should be utilized with regard to these limited duration estates.[19] A life estate entitles one to a limited title to real property for only so long as the person lives. While sometimes property subject to a life estate can be transferred to another person, the interest is automatically extinguished upon the death of the person referenced in the original life estate. There are also conditional or defeasible estates, whereby title is extinguished upon a particular occurrence or happening. Such estates can be subject to a condition precedent or a condition subsequent. The type of conditional estate involved can have different legal implications. A right of reverter, a power of termination, a right of entry, and similar matters are complex legal traits associated with certain conditional estates. In Michigan, certain future estates can also be created.

It is always important for a purchaser to ascertain what type of title is desired before the closing and to provide for the granting of such title in the purchase/sales agreement.

Footnotes

[19] The purchaser certainly should consult with his or her attorney regarding these matters.

Chapter 23
"TAKING TITLE"

ONE ASPECT OF A REAL ESTATE TRANSACTION THAT purchasers often overlook is how the property will be "titled" once the purchaser owns the property; that is, should the deed grant title for the property to a person, more than one person, a married couple, a trust, a partnership, a corporation or LLC, or some other entity? This matter should be settled prior to closing so that the final deed or land contract will accurately reflect the purchaser's preference.

For individuals, the "grantee" in a deed (normally, the purchaser) can be one person, two persons, or multiple persons. If a deed is to be titled in the name of a single person, the status of that person should normally be noted in the deed (for example, the deed should indicate that the property transfers to "Michael Smith, a single man" or "Michelle Brown, an unmarried woman"). Michigan still has the old-fashioned common law "dower" interest for married women. Accordingly, even if a married man is listed as the only grantee in a deed, his wife will still automatically own a share of the property (even though she is not mentioned in the deed) pursuant to her dower right. Typically, if the grantees in a deed are a married couple, they will take any property as "tenants by the entireties." Ideally, the deed should indicate that the married couple is taking title as tenants by the entireties, although even without the entireties language, the law normally presumes that a married couple will take title to a property as tenants by the entireties. A tenancy by the entireties is merely one type of joint tenancy in Michigan. With an entireties tenancy, should one spouse die, the other spouse automatically has the rights as the survivor and takes title to the overall property.

Two or more individuals can be listed on a deed as the grantees (purchasers) pursuant to two different types of joint tenancies. If the grantees on the deed are listed as taking title as "tenants in common," each of the grantees will take an undivided equal interest in the whole of the property. When a common tenant dies, the surviving grantee (or grantees) does not automatically obtain the deceased tenant's share. Rather, the deceased tenant's share can pass by the deceased tenant's will or trust, by contract, or otherwise. If a deed lists two or more grantees as "joint tenants with the right of survivorship" (or equivalent language), should one of the property owners die, the other joint tenant or tenants automatically receives the deceased tenant's share.

Major risks and potentially unforeseen consequences can result from the careless use of either a tenancy in common or tenancy with rights of survivorship. Where two or more individuals own a property jointly as common tenants, the situation can often prove unworkable, particularly if there is no written side agreement regarding how the property will be utilized, maintained, sold, transferred, etc. A tenancy with a right of survivorship can result in horrifically unfair consequences, depending upon which tenant dies first. The remaining surviving owner or owners can receive a windfall. The surviving tenant or tenants receive the ownership share of the deceased property owner without having to pay any money to the deceased property owner's estate, spouse, or family. Parents sometimes add their children to title to real property via a deed naming the children as tenants in common or joint tenants with the right of survivorship as a way of doing estate planning "on the cheap." Almost always, that technique is a bad idea for many reasons (for example, the parents later wish to sell the property but one or more children refuse to agree to the sale, a creditor attaches the interest of one of the children, a former son-in-law obtains an interest in the property through a divorce proceeding, etc.).

A deed can also cause waterfront property to be titled in the name of a trust, corporation, limited liability company, or other entity. Quite often, there are tax or estate planning reasons for placing the title to a waterfront property in the name of a trust, limited liability company, or other entity.

The prospective purchaser of a lakefront property should always consult with a competent real estate or estate planning attorney regarding title matters.

Chapter 24
POSSESSION

SOMETIME AT OR AFTER CLOSING, THE SELLER WILL have to give up possession of the property and the buyer will take possession. Both the seller and the buyer should preplan the practical aspects leading up to the "handoff" of possession.

It is often prudent to have the parties do a "walkthrough" of the property or dwelling a day or two before closing to ascertain the condition of the property (particularly if the buyer's property inspection occurred a while ago), verify the contents of the dwelling, and deal with any last-minute or unforeseen issues.

Some of the matters that should be arranged (or persons or firms notified) prior to the buyer obtaining possession (and be effective at the moment the buyer takes possession) include the following:

- Electric (the premises should be removed from the seller's name and placed in the buyer's name).
- Water and sewer (contact the local municipality where applicable).
- Natural gas company, or alternately, the propane supply company.
- Cable television company, or alternately, the satellite dish company.

- Local tax assessor (although the paperwork will eventually catch up with the municipal tax assessor, sometimes it is prudent to let him/her know right away).

- Lake association, where applicable.

- Telephone company.

- Garbage pickup company or the municipal garbage pickup department.

- Private road association, where applicable.

- Have homeowners insurance (theft, fire, liability, etc.) and other insurance in place.

- Obtaining the keys and codes (if any) for a dwelling, although they should be changed soon after possession.

Both the seller and the buyer will want to make sure that the above matters are resolved at or prior to the time that the buyer takes possession so that the liability of one does not potentially implicate the other. In addition, it is normally prudent for the buyer to have all of the keys and exterior locks changed on any dwelling or accessory building. Even in a situation where the buyer knows and trusts the seller, it is possible that the seller may have given keys to a variety of family members, repair technicians, etc., in the past.

Chapter 25
ZONING AND OTHER LOCAL ORDINANCES AND STATE REGULATIONS AFFECTING WATERFRONT PROPERTY

BEFORE PURCHASING WATERFRONT PROPERTY, PART of the due diligence process that a prospective purchaser should follow (including placing a relevant contingency clause in the purchase/sales agreement) involves a thorough investigation of the applicability of local zoning regulations, other local ordinances, and potentially even state environmental regulations regarding the property. If a prospective purchaser intends to build a new cottage or dwelling (or add onto an existing one), divide the land, install a new seawall or permanent dock, fill in a portion of the property, or engage in similar undertakings, it is essential that the prospective purchaser research all relevant local and state regulations beforehand to ensure that such construction or undertaking can lawfully occur after the property is purchased.

Michigan does have a somewhat confusing patchwork of multi-level government regulations, including regarding the waterfront. At the state level, there are generally two types of laws that can regulate the use and alteration of waterfront property. The first type of statewide laws are environmental in nature, and regulate matters such as dredging in bodies of water, filling wetlands or other bodies of water, building in or altering sand dunes around the Great Lakes, installing or expanding seawalls, sanding beaches, installing permanent docks, and installing seasonal docks (and similar structures) on the Great Lakes and certain inland lakes tied into the Great Lakes. The second general area of state regulation involves Michigan boating laws.

In general, statutes and regulations at the state level in Michigan do not extensively regulate dockage, permanent boat moorage, the intensity of development on the lakeshore, and similar matters. Other states have regulatory schemes at the state level that are much more comprehensive regarding the waterfront than Michigan.

Regulations regarding the waterfront at the county level are quite sparse. County health departments do regulate the installation and maintenance of private septic systems and wells on lakefront properties. A few counties have adopted fertilizer regulations or bans for waterfront property. In areas where there is no township, city, or village zoning, few counties have adopted county zoning. Except for those limited examples, however, county regulation of the waterfront is quite limited.

If you are planning on purchasing a waterfront property in Michigan, the unit of government that will most likely constrain what you want to do on and with your lakefront property is the local government. In Michigan, the local government is either a city, village, or township. Townships are the "default" form of local government in Michigan; that is, if a particular area has not been incorporated as a city or village, it is located within a township. Local governments in Michigan have extensive powers to adopt and enforce ordinances regarding a variety of different topics, including the waterfront. Local ordinances tend to be of two types. First, a city, village, or township can adopt zoning regulations pursuant to the Michigan Zoning Enabling Act, being MCL 125.3101 *et seq*. In addition, local governments in Michigan are authorized to adopt nonzoning ordinances (often referred to as "standalone" or police power ordinances). Such ordinances can also regulate lakefront properties and the waterfront. Zoning regulations tend to be concerned with the use of land and the waterfront, whereas police power ordinances tend to regulate actions or activities.

The violation of a municipal ordinance in Michigan can either constitute a criminal misdemeanor upon conviction (punishable by up to 93 days in jail, the imposition of a $500.00 fine, or both) or a municipal civil infraction offense (no jail time, but there can be fines, court orders, and municipal reimbursement imposed).

The overwhelming majority of municipalities in Michigan where lakes are located have a local municipal zoning ordinance. Zoning ordinances vary dramatically, both with regard to their length and the subjects covered. Most zoning ordinances, however, severely impact the ability of a riparian property owner to do what he or she desires with a waterfront property.

Following are some examples of the potential reach of local zoning regulations. Have you always wanted to build the lakefront cottage of your dreams, with a walkout basement and peak roof that towers some 40 feet over the base of the walkout area? You will not be able to construct a dwelling that large if the local zoning regulations limit the height of new dwellings (or additions to new dwellings) to 30 feet. How is the height of a dwelling measured in the local zoning ordinance—from the lowest point of the building to the tallest point of the building? From the tallest point of the building to the average grade around the building? To the median point of the roof? It all depends on the language of the local ordinance. A riparian may want to add on to an existing cottage, but cannot do so because it would violate the side yard setback requirements. Another riparian proposes to add a deck onto the lakefront side of her cottage, but is not able to do so, since a deck is considered a "structure" for purposes of the local zoning regulations and the setback from the lake is 75 feet. What if a riparian wants to construct a detached garage with a "relative's apartment" above? Many zoning ordinances prohibit that.

Some riparian properties are large enough such that a prospective purchaser would like to divide the property after closing and sell one or more new lots to finance the purchase. Of course, small waterfront properties normally cannot be split or divided. However, with regard to waterfront properties of a significant size, many prospective purchasers convince themselves that they will be able to afford the waterfront property based on a plan to carve off one or more smaller waterfront parcels to sell after the property is obtained. Never simply assume, however, that a waterfront lot or parcel can be split—there are many laws and ordinances that might make such a property split or division difficult or even impossible.

Platted lots cannot be split or divided (or their platted boundary lines changed) unless an expensive replat occurs or the local municipality has a review and approval process that is completed by the landowner. See MCL 560.263. Unplatted parcels cannot be split or divided except in compliance with the Michigan

Land Division Act (MCL 560.101 *et seq.*) and such divisions are subject to approval by the local municipality (often under a local ordinance). See MCL 560.109 *et seq.* Even if an unplatted lakefront lot can lawfully be split or divided pursuant to state statute or local ordinances, unless the seller grants the buyer the number of land division "rights" necessary (as specified by the Michigan Land Division Act) in the deed or land contract, the property division or split cannot occur absent going through the expensive platting or site condominium process. Condominium units cannot be split or altered without formal condominium association approval and perhaps even a formal master deed amendment (and, of course, local municipal approval). Finally, if the waterfront property is subject to deed restrictions/restrictive covenants, there might be a prohibition on property splits or land divisions.

Some zoning regulations contain a "buffer" or "greenbelt" area requirement mandating that all existing trees and natural vegetation within so many feet of a body of water (50 feet, for example) must remain undisturbed, except for a 30-foot-wide access and use strip. While that might not affect existing lawns or properties with a dwelling (which are lawfully nonconforming or "grandparented"), such regulations could severely limit the options of someone who buys vacant waterfront property and wants to build a new dwelling. What if you purchase a waterfront property that has access to a public road by an easement, but the private road has not been installed? Local zoning regulations could make the installation of a private road very expensive. These are just a few examples of how local zoning regulations can adversely affect the options of a waterfront property purchaser.

In addition to municipal zoning regulations, a number of municipalities have nonzoning (or "police power") ordinance provisions that can also impact waterfront properties. Such ordinances can cover a variety of different topics including fertilizer bans on waterfront properties, sand dune protection, limitations on the number, type, and placement of docks, rafts, boat cradles, and watercraft, RV and off-season boat storage rules, flood area restrictions, local wetlands regulations, and even limits on which trees can be removed!

Given that most waterfront properties are located in rural areas where municipal water and sewer may not be available, dwellings in those areas must rely on private wells and individual septic systems.[20] Typically, county health department regulations

govern septic system and well installations or alterations. A very
important contingency that should be inserted into a purchase/
sales agreement is a clause that allows a prospective purchaser to
back out of the deal if testing done between the date of the signing
of the purchase/sales agreement and closing indicates that the
property is not suitable for a private well or private septic system,
or that the installation (or upgrading) of either system would be
prohibitively expensive. Typically, testing for private septic systems
is done by the local health department. In the past, septic tests were
often referred to as "perk" tests, although the tests used today are
different. The installation (or expansion) of private septic systems
can be expensive, particularly if soil and topography limitations
require the installation and use of more expensive "raised mound"
or aerobic septic systems.[21]

State regulations can also severely impact the ability of a
riparian to build a new or replacement dwelling, add on to an
existing dwelling, replace or install a seawall, fill a wetlands,
dredge the shore, or engage in similar waterfront property projects.
For example, no seawall can be rebuilt or installed, no permanent
dock installed, and no lake dredging or similar activities can
occur without prior approval by one or more state agencies. If the
riparian property is located within a critical dune area pursuant
to the Michigan Dune Protection Act (MCL 324.35301 *et seq.*),
buildings and structures cannot be built, installed, or expanded
without prior approval by one or more state agencies. In addition,
on the Great Lakes, structures cannot be installed, shoreline erosion
devices cannot be built, docks and boat hoists cannot be installed,
and many other undertakings cannot occur near the water without
the approval of one or more state agencies, as well as potentially,
the United States Army Corps of Engineers and the Environmental
Protection Agency. Please see Chapter 27 for a more in-depth
discussion of state regulations that impact waterfront uses.

The prospective purchaser of a waterfront property who does
not fully complete his or her due diligence with regard to local,
state, and federal regulations before purchasing a waterfront
property can find their use options for that property severely
limited after closing. In fact, in some extreme cases, a vacant
waterfront property may prove to be totally "unbuildable" based
on one or more local, state, county health department, and/or
federal regulations. Placing the appropriate contingency language
in the purchase/sales agreement before signing regarding these
matters (and doing the due diligence before closing) is essential.

Footnotes

[20] Many municipalities with public water or sewer require mandatory hookup if new construction is to be located within a certain distance of a sewer or water main.

[21] A prospective buyer should also familiarize himself or herself with the on-site septic system for an existing cottage or dwelling. It is important to know exactly where the septic system and drain field are located and what type of system exists. A history of maintenance of the septic system is also important to know, including when sewage has been pumped out of the system. It is normally prudent to have a septic system inspector review the existing septic system before closing, as well as have a contingency clause in the purchase/sales agreement regarding the sufficiency of the existing septic system.

Chapter 26
"BUILDABILITY"

PROSPECTIVE PURCHASERS OF WATERFRONT property should realize that not all vacant waterfront property is "buildable." More than a few people in Michigan have purchased the vacant lakefront property of their dreams, only to find out after the purchase that no dwelling or cottage can be built on the lakefront parcel and that the land is only good for occasional visits.

The lawful status of a lakefront property under a local municipal zoning ordinance or other municipal ordinance is not a guarantee (or sometimes, even an indication) of "buildability." When a person creates a lot or parcel via a land division (and receives a property tax identification number), that is no guarantee of buildability. Furthermore, purchase/sales agreements and deeds (or land contracts) given by a seller of waterfront property are almost never guarantees or representations of buildability.[22] Finally, title insurance does not guarantee or even indicate the buildability of vacant waterfront parcels. When dealing with all waterfront properties, but particularly vacant waterfront properties, *caveat emptor* ("buyer beware") is particularly applicable.

Some of the same pitfalls associated with building a cottage or dwelling on a vacant lakefront property are also applicable if a prospective purchaser wishes to remove an existing cottage or dwelling on the property and build a new dwelling or to add onto an existing dwelling.

One of the first matters that a prospective purchaser of waterfront property should consider is the physical characteristics of the land and its suitability for building or expanding a dwelling. Physical suitability for building involves a variety of different factors and considerations. For example, waterfront parcels without natural gas will normally have to be served with propane. Waterfront property owners must ensure that there is at least one location on-site where a large propane tank can be installed and that the propane company will be able to access that tank to regularly fill it up.

Portions of some waterfront properties are located within a flood zone, floodplain, or the 100-year flood area. In some instances, that may preclude buildability altogether (either practically, or due to a local ordinance or state or federal regulation, or statutory prohibition), while in other situations, it could mean being able to build a dwelling (or add on to an existing dwelling) but the property owner will have to obtain (and maintain) expensive annual flood insurance. High water levels due to naturally fluctuating water levels (or due to lake level control items such as dams or lake augmentation wells) can preclude basements for lakefront dwellings, cause lawn flooding, create shoreline erosion, and present similar problems.

One common problem with waterfront lots (particularly in subdivisions or heavily-developed areas) is property drainage or stormwater runoff. Is the waterfront property you are considering buying subject to flooding due to runoff from an adjoining parcel? Does the lot you are considering dump stormwater onto an adjoining lot? Is there standing water on the lot when it rains? Does an official county drain traverse or adjoin the property? Are there drainage easements? Drainage issues are often very significant with waterfront properties. An engineer can help identify and potentially resolve drainage and stormwater runoff problems.

Some waterfront properties are not suitable for basements or walkout levels.

If no public water or sanitary sewer is available for the property, a private well and septic system will have to be installed for any new dwelling (and sometimes for an expanded dwelling). In Michigan, on occasion, there are waterfront properties that are not suitable for on-site private septic systems or private water wells. The waterfront property owner will not be able to obtain a building permit for the construction of a new dwelling (and sometimes for an expanded dwelling) if the appropriate approvals and permits cannot be obtained for both a suitable on-site water well and septic system. Private septic systems can sometimes be a particularly knotty problem for waterfront properties. Not only must the soils on-site be suitable for a private septic and drain field, but numerous setbacks will also have to be met for the system itself. For example, most county health departments require that a septic system be located a significant distance away from the ordinary high water mark of a body of water, as well as specified distances away from all lot lines, the road, the dwelling itself and other adjoining dwellings (if any), the on-site well (or wells on other properties), and other items. In some cases, the local health department will not approve a conventional septic system for a waterfront property, but will allow an alternate system such as an aerobic system or a raised mound system. Unfortunately, those systems tend to be significantly more expensive than conventional septic systems. Finally, drain fields for septic systems often must be large and can take up a significant portion of a waterfront lot. Some health departments require a "backup" or "reserve" drain field area on site just in case the primary drain field ever fails.

Extending electrical lines, telephone lines, and natural gas to a waterfront building site can be both expensive and difficult. For example, can such utilities be run entirely within your property or will you have to obtain utility easements from one or more neighbors? What is the cost of running a new line? Are there additional utility fees charged due to the property being in a rural area? Are there frequent power outages in the area?

Sometimes, unbeknown to a prospective purchaser, waterfront properties have been built up by significant fill in the past. That can adversely affect the buildability of a new or expanded dwelling and the requirement that new construction must rest on firm ground. Some waterfront sites are composed of clay or mucky soils, which can make building difficult and more expensive.

Many waterfront properties have wetlands. Wetlands cannot be filled or altered without prior approval and a permit from the state of Michigan (and the U.S. Army Corps of Engineers in some cases), and in some municipalities, the local municipal government. On some waterfront properties, the type and extent of wetlands involved may preclude building a dwelling (or expanding or replacing an existing dwelling) altogether.

On rare occasions, a waterfront property will prove unbuildable due to the presence of protected plant species, unstable soils or ground, extensive springs, or other factors on site. Severe slopes on a waterfront property can preclude buildability (as well as prevent the use of an on-site septic system) or at the very least, make building a dwelling very challenging and expensive.

In many cases, the purchaser of a waterfront property will not be able to build as large a dwelling as desired (or the accessory buildings that the purchaser envisioned) due to the limited size of the waterfront parcel, setbacks, the physical attributes of the property, or local zoning regulations.

Many prospective purchasers of a waterfront property never examine the beach, water, or bottomlands of a lake or river adjacent to the property involved before the purchase, either because the purchase transaction occurs in the winter or they do not think of it. There are many beautiful waterfront properties in Michigan that have waterfront and bottomlands problems due to erosion, muck, jagged rocks and stones, or similar conditions that make use of the waterfront less desirable.

Local zoning regulations can potentially prevent a waterfront property from being "buildable" or make building a dwelling more expensive and challenging, as well as potentially preclude the owner's ability to replace an existing dwelling or to add onto an existing dwelling. Most zoning regulations contain required setbacks for buildings and all portions of buildings (normally, this includes decks, roof overhangs, etc.) from property lines, the waterfront, the road, and other buildings. Most zoning regulations contain height limitations for new or expanded dwellings. Some zoning regulations contain a limit on how much of a waterfront lot can be covered with impervious surfaces such as buildings, decks, sidewalks, paved or cement driveways, and similar items. A few municipalities have regulations that specify setback requirements for wells and septic systems from buildings, structures, lot lines, the waterfront, and other wells, and such regulations can be in addition to the setback requirements specified by the local health department.

Many waterfront property owners who have faced local zoning regulations that make buildability difficult or even impossible have simply assumed that they will be able to obtain a variance from the local government's zoning board of appeals with regard to setbacks, height, and other zoning requirements. In actuality, such variances are normally difficult to obtain and no prospective waterfront property owner should assume ahead of time that a variance will be granted.

In addition to conventional zoning regulations, there are a variety of other local ordinance provisions (sometimes contained in the local zoning ordinance and sometimes located outside of the zoning ordinance in another ordinance) that can impact the buildability (or "usability") of a waterfront parcel. Some municipalities have green belt or buffer regulations that not only preclude building within a certain distance from the waterfront, but also prohibit the cutting of trees, foliage, and vegetation within a certain specified distance of the body of water involved. Although not a matter of buildability *per se*, many municipalities with lakes and rivers have zoning or other regulations that regulate the type, size, and location of docks, the number of boats that a given waterfront property owner can keep, the type of water rafts allowed, and similar waterfront regulations. Some municipalities have ordinance provisions that regulate buildability near wetlands, within flood areas, within sand dune areas, and on slopes over a certain grade. Many municipalities have private road regulations that require the installation of expensive private roads for waterfront property without frontage on a public road and will not issue a building permit for a new or expanded dwelling until the required private road has been installed or upgraded. Generally, a new driveway cannot be installed without a county or local government driveway (or curb cut) permit.

While certain area characteristics do not preclude buildability, they can make the waterfront property less desirable. Such negative factors can include:

- A nearby landfill or airport
- An adjoining farm (where noises, smells, and similar irritants are protected by the Michigan Right to Farm Act)
- Nearby commercial or industrial uses
- Nearby water access sites (road ends, alleys, parks, easements, etc.)

- A nearby expressway
- A nearby state park or campground
- A vacant property that could be developed (or overdeveloped) in the future

Such matters should be fully investigated <u>before</u> you are obligated to close on the waterfront property involved.

Footnotes

[22] In fact, unless the seller of a property gives a rare optional guarantee of buildability, there is no such guarantee or warranty under Michigan law.

Chapter 27
RELEVANT MICHIGAN STATUTES THAT AFFECT THE WATERFRONT

UNFORTUNATELY, WATERFRONT PROPERTY OWNERS not only have to be concerned about local city, village, or township ordinances (for example, zoning ordinances, police power ordinances, fertilizer ordinances, dock ordinances, natural buffer strip ordinances, etc.) and county health codes (well and septic regulations, potential fertilizer bans, etc.), but also state environmental statutes regarding certain improvements on a waterfront lot or alterations in the water. And, if the waterfront property is on one of the Great Lakes or a major navigable river, federal environmental statutes may also apply.

The following are some Michigan statutes that can pertain to uses, structures, buildings, alterations, construction, and projects at or near the waterfront:[23]

- The Michigan Wetland Protection Act (MCL 324.30301 *et seq.*)
- The Inland Lakes and Streams Act (MCL 324.30101 *et seq.*)
- The Michigan Sand Dune Protection and Management Act (MCL 324.35301 *et seq.*)
- The Marine Safety Act (MCL 324.80101 *et seq.*)
- The Soil Erosion and Sedimentation Act (MCL 324.9101 *et seq.*)
- The Great Lakes Submerged Lands Act (MCL 324.32501 *et seq.*)

- The Natural Rivers Act (MCL 324.30501 *et seq.*)
- The Inland Lake Level Act of 1961 (MCL 324.30701 *et seq.*)
- The Inland Lake Improvement Act (MCL 324.30901 *et seq.*)

Where the above statutes apply, a construction project, structure, building, alteration, use, or activity normally cannot be commenced until the landowner has filed the appropriate application or applications with one or more state agencies and the necessary permit(s) or approval(s) have been obtained. Failure to comply with those statutes can result in severe financial and even potentially criminal penalties.

Before you purchased your dream waterfront parcel, you began making plans for altering the land or the shoreline. Those plans could have included filling in a low-lying area (which you are just certain must not be wetlands), dredging mucky bottomlands in what will be your swim area, replacing a broken down seawall, putting sand on the beach (and a little way out into the water), or filling in "spongy" areas near the shoreline. Although you may have assumed before you purchased the waterfront property that you could do some or all of these projects once you own the land, one or more federal or state statutes (or even local ordinances) may severely curtail or even preclude your project. Unfortunately, now that you own your dream property, you may not be able to actually have those projects done due to state or federal laws.[24]

If you are dealing with an inland lake, river, or stream in Michigan (and which does not have direct access to one of the Great Lakes), it is likely that you will be working with the Michigan Department of Natural Resources and the Environment ("DNRE")[25] regarding these projects. Wetlands cannot be filled or altered without a permit from the DNRE pursuant to the Michigan Wetland Protection Act. In addition, lands that sometimes appear not to be wetlands frequently are. With an inland lake in Michigan, no alterations can occur in the water or even "lakeward" of the ordinary high water mark without the appropriate permit from the DNRE. Projects that require such a permit include, but are not necessarily limited to, dredging, filling, installing or replacing seawalls, placement of sand, the installation of a permanent dock, and other activities. While theoretically, you can alter nondune land that is "uplands" from the ordinary high water mark of a lake, stream, river, or creek without a state permit (you may need a local one, however), you cannot do so in such a fashion that it will "migrate" down into the water.

If your project will involve one of the Great Lakes or an inland lake directly tied into one of the Great Lakes, you will likely be dealing with both the U.S. Army Corps of Engineers and the DNRE. Generally, some or all of the state statutes listed above apply (as well as potentially, local ordinances), but certain federal statutes may also come into play. In most cases, the U.S. Army Corps of Engineers and the DNRE have reciprocity agreements where if you first apply to one agency, that agency will process the permit application and forward the necessary paperwork to the other agency for final approval.

Do not assume that obtaining the necessary permit or permits for some of these projects will be an easy process. Quite often, permit applications are turned down. In some cases, the landowner can scale back their proposal, resubmit their request, and obtain a more modest permit. Sometimes, receiving a permit can take a significant period of time. It is also often prudent to hire a professional consultant who can assist with the permit application, review, and approval process. It is common for such consultants to be former officials or employees of the U.S. Army Corps of Engineers or DNRE, so that they "speak the language" of those agencies. They also typically know what the government agency is inclined to approve and what will not pass muster.

For a checklist regarding obstacles and permit requirements for the installation of docks, seawalls, and buildings at the lakefront, please see Attachment K.

Footnotes

[23] Many of the statutes mentioned on this page have been listed by their common or former names. The statutes are now part of the Michigan Natural Resources and Environmental Protection Act, such that those statute names do not technically apply anymore. Nevertheless, it is helpful to use the common former names.

[24] As the old saying goes, do not assume, as it makes an "a**" out of "u" and "me."

[25] The Michigan department or agency that as of early 2011 was known as the "Department of Natural Resources and the Environment." During most of the 1990s and 2000s, it was two different departments or agencies called the "Department of Natural Resources" and the "Department of Environmental Quality" that were combined in 2010. If the Department of Natural Resources and the Environment is hereafter split or reorganized (which appears likely), the phrase "Department of Natural Resources and the Environment" or "DNRE" in this publication shall mean the applicable Michigan agency, agencies, commission, or commissions.

Chapter 28
ACCESSIBILITY

ACCESSIBILITY TO A WATERFRONT PROPERTY IS OFTEN
a key issue. Where a vacant waterfront property has frontage
on a public road, the owner must ensure that the driveway can
be physically installed from the public road to the building site
and that the governmental unit with jurisdiction over the public
road will issue a driveway curb cut permit. Also, just because
a public road right-of-way is involved does not mean that any
governmental unit maintains the road or plows it in the winter.
"Seasonal" public roads receive little maintenance in Michigan. If
the waterfront property does not have frontage on a public road,
many (but not all) municipalities will allow a shared driveway
or private road, although subject to various regulations. In some
instances, joint driveways and private roads will need local
municipal approval. In some cases, the installation of such a joint
driveway or private road can be expensive due to municipal
private road construction standards or topographical limitations.
Existing private roads or joint drives can also present a host of
problems. Many such access easements are narrow or substandard.
Some are ill-defined. Others are poorly maintained. Some access
easements do not allow utility lines to be located within the
easement. Many private roads or joint drives do not have a good
recorded maintenance agreement that sets up procedures for road
maintenance, sharing costs, voting procedures for major decisions,

and snowplowing. The lack of a good binding private road maintenance agreement can make some mortgage lenders nervous. Private roads often breed conflicts among users.

There may also be legal obstacles to installing (or upgrading) a joint driveway or private road based on the presence of wetlands, sand dunes (which may be protected by the Michigan Dune Protection Act), and similar issues. Do not just assume that lawful and easy access to a waterfront property already exists or can be obtained later — investigate first!

If a waterfront parcel or lot does not have frontage on a public road, Michigan law (MCL 560.261) requires that the seller disclose in writing that fact and the following: "The street or road abutted by this property is private and is not required to be maintained by the _X_ County Road Commission."

Chapter 29
WATERFRONT PROPERTY TAXES AND ASSESSMENTS

AFTER I PURCHASE A WATERFRONT PROPERTY IN Michigan, what will my property tax bill be for the next year? Typically, when you purchase real property in Michigan, the taxable value (the value of the property against which the tax rate is applied) is "uncapped" and can result in a dramatic increase in property taxes, as discussed further below. Therefore, before purchasing a waterfront property, the current tax assessment and amount of annual property taxes for the property should be carefully reviewed.

Under Proposal A (which was adopted by Michigan voters in 1994), so long as a particular property owner owns a property in Michigan, the taxable value of the property for a given year can not increase by more than 5% of the taxable value for the prior year or the rate of inflation, whichever is less. Accordingly, property taxes for a particular property cannot effectively increase by more than 5% or the rate of inflation for a given year (whichever is less) so long as the property is not sold or transferred (with some exceptions). Once a property is sold, the cap comes off and the taxable value (as well as the amount of the annual property taxes) is typically "reset."

While the taxable value assigned to the property before it was sold can be quite low (particularly if the prior landowner owned the waterfront property for a long period of time, such that the market value greatly outpaced the rate of inflation or 5%, whichever was less as applied on an annual basis), it will almost always "pop up" in the year following the sale. The new taxable value for your property (the "reset" valuation) should be fairly close to one-half of the fair market value of the property, which almost always results in a dramatic increase in the property taxes. It is possible that the new taxable value will be slightly more than half of what you paid for the property (if the local municipal tax assessor believes that you received a bargain price) or even less than one-half of what you paid (if the municipal tax assessor believes that you "overpaid" for the property). Your tax bill will be much less if your new dwelling is your declared "homestead" under Michigan law (your permanent primary residence) than if you do not or cannot list it as your homestead (that is, your primary residence is elsewhere or the land is vacant).

In general, property taxes for waterfront properties tend to be higher than for similar conventional properties given that waterfront properties are more valuable. Furthermore, there is often a mild "bias" by some local municipal and tax assessing authorities with regard to waterfront properties based on the fact that many waterfront property owners are not residents, and thus, are not local voters. This is not true in most municipalities (as the assessors for most municipalities are fair and professional), but in some municipalities such biases are subtle and oftentimes unintentional.

An important matter to consider with regard to real property taxes is the allocation or proration of such taxes at closing. The purchaser of a waterfront property will want to ensure that all outstanding real property taxes (as well as any other liens or encumbrances on the waterfront property) are paid in full at or prior to closing so that the purchaser will obtain title to the property after closing, free and clear of all outstanding real property taxes and other liens and encumbrances. The purchase/ sales agreement should deal with the allocation (*i.e.,* splitting) of real property taxes at closing as described in Chapter 19.

On occasion, a waterfront property will be subject to a multi-year additional tax called a "special assessment." Such assessments "run with the land" and continue even after a change of ownership. A special assessment is a method for the local government to finance a service or improvement such as aquatic weed treatments for the lake, street lighting, sidewalks, a new municipal sanitary sewer system, or extra police patrols.

*   *   *

A Property Tax Assessment and Appeals Mini-Course

In Michigan, annual property taxes for land (and any dwellings or certain other improvements thereon) are based on a formula. The millage rate is the percentage formula applied by the local taxing authority. One unit of millage is often referred to as a "mill." Millage rates vary dramatically, depending upon the unit of government involved. Cities tend to have the highest millage rates (due to the significant number of services provided), while townships usually have the lowest millage rates (due to typically limited services). Village millages often are in between. The local unit of government (a city, township, or village) collects not only the property taxes based upon its own millage rates, but also property taxes for other units of government (for example, state, county, school, library, and other applicable units of government).

In order to determine the applicable annual property tax for a given piece of property, the local government tax assessor must first figure out what the property is worth (what it would sell for in a free market, arms-length transaction). A local municipal tax assessor redetermines the value of each property in the unit of government involved on an annual basis. How is that done? The tax assessor must consider a variety of different factors, including comparable sales, certain state formulas, any on-site improvements, additions, or deletions during the prior year, and geographic and economic factors. In Michigan, waterfront property owners typically receive two different annual tax bills—a "winter" tax bill (generally received in early December), and a "summer" tax bill (typically received in July). In most jurisdictions, the summer tax bill tends to be larger than the winter tax bill.

In actuality, the local tax assessor must come up with two different property tax valuations or assessments for each property every year. The first annual tax assessment is referred to as the "assessed value." The assessed value constitutes one-half (50%) of the assessor's best judgment as to the fair market value of a given piece of property in a particular year. Prior to 1995, the assessed value was the only valuation tracked by local governments and it was simply multiplied by the millage rate to obtain the property tax bill. However, in 1994, the voters in Michigan approved

Proposal A, which created a new property tax scheme, as well as something called "taxable value." Generally, in order to determine the annual property tax, the taxable value of a given parcel is multiplied times the millage rate (for example, a city levying a total millage of 20 mills means a rate or multiplier of 2% or $20.00 of tax for every $1,000 of property value as assessed) in order to obtain the property tax amount.

Under Proposal A (which is still in effect today), the taxable value of a given property cannot increase by more than 5% or the rate of inflation (whichever is less) on an annual basis. That "cap" is in effect as long as the same property owner owns the land involved, does not add a building or significant improvements to the property, and does not take any action that constitutes a "transfer of ownership" under the Michigan General Property Tax Act. Taxable value is that "capped" or limited annual tax assessment.

Proposal A has effectively created a two-tier property tax valuation/assessment system in Michigan. Waterfront property owners who have owned their riparian property for long periods of time have seen their taxable values grow (and, hence, their property taxes) much more slowly over time than the owners of riparian properties that change ownership frequently. Overall, Proposal A has been a true friend to riparian property owners throughout Michigan who held onto their land for long periods of time as waterfront properties have tended to increase in value over the last decade and a half much more rapidly than nonwaterfront properties.

Every property owner in Michigan receives an annual notification of the change to the property tax assessments for each piece of property owned. That notice lists or "tracks" two different assessments (or property valuations) — "taxable value" and "assessed value." Remember, the assessed value is the free-floating valuation that supposedly follows market value. Taxable value is the "capped" valuation that, absent a transfer of ownership or other "triggers," could not have increased annually by more than 5% or the rate of inflation (whichever was less). Until recently, the assessed value for a given piece of riparian property was significantly higher than the taxable value due to the appreciation of waterfront properties over the years where one landowner is involved.

From 1995 to about 2007, assessed value probably mattered little to most property owners who continued to own their properties after Proposal A. Taxable value was what really mattered, as taxable value was the amount to which the millage rate was applied to obtain the actual property tax owed. Once a property was sold, the taxable value "uncapped" or "popped up" to what the assessed value was at the time of sale (generally 50% of the fair market value). Accordingly, over the past 15 years or so, fewer property owners challenged or appealed annual increases in the assessed value as it was seen as a somewhat meaningless number.

A few property owners did continue to challenge annual assessed value increases, even where their taxable value was considerably less than the assessed value. Why? First, some landowners believed that a high assessed value would potentially scare away purchasers of the property, as it was likely that once the property was sold, the taxable value would "uncap" or "pop up" to the assessed value. However, most prospective purchasers knew that anyway. Second, some property owners simply did not understand the difference between taxable value and assessed value. Finally, some sophisticated property owners foresaw a potential time when property values might fall, and the quicker that assessed value fell below taxable value, the quicker one's property taxes would decrease. Taxable value never falls (even during years that actual property values fall) until and unless the assessed value falls to the level of the taxable value and decreases further. Once assessed value and taxable value "meet," taxable value will fall together with assessed value beyond that point. There is effectively a "ratchet down" effect—when assessed value falls below taxable value, taxable value is decreased down to that valuation and a new "cap" is set.

Something has happened the last few years in Michigan that the drafters of Proposal A did not envision—deflation or decreasing property values on a massive scale.

A lakefront property owner can appeal his/her annual property tax assessments, but can only do so once a year, and any such appeal must be pursued exactly as required by law. In general, property taxpayers in Michigan receive three notices per year from the local taxing authority regarding property taxes. Two of those notices are simply property tax bills, which are generally received by the landowner in early December (for the winter property tax bill) and June (for the summer property tax bill). The third annual notice is the notice of assessment, which the property owner typically receives in late February or March. It is that last notice (the property tax assessment adjustment notice) that the landowner must carefully review to determine whether or not to appeal the property tax assessments (valuations) for that tax year. A landowner has a relatively narrow window time period within which to file a formal appeal once the notice of assessment has been received.

Typically, the initial assessment appeal must be made by a landowner to the local government's board of review which meets during March shortly after the new property tax assessment notice has been received. A property owner can either appear in person at the meeting of the local board of review or file a written appeal in a timely fashion before the board of review meets. If the landowner disagrees with the decision by the local board of review, the landowner must promptly file a further written appeal with the Michigan Tax Tribunal.

It should always be remembered that a local board of review (and the Tax Tribunal if a further appeal occurs) has the authority to keep the reassessment as is, decrease the property tax assessment, or (and this is what some property owners forget) actually increase the property tax assessment if an error was made.

Property tax assessment appeals may be advantageous to an unusually large number of lakefront property owners at this time. If lakefront property values in your area have fallen significantly, you may be able to argue that your assessed value has fallen so low that your taxable value should decrease also. Or, even if the local tax assessor has lowered both your assessed value and taxable value, there may be a reasonable argument for further reductions. Remember, once lakefront property values begin to rise again as the economy improves (whenever that might occur in Michigan!), the assessed value and the taxable value will both begin to increase again. Accordingly, it is normally to the benefit of a lakefront property owner to have the taxable value "reset" as low as possible now so that future annual valuation increases will be operating off of a lower reset base.

Why are both taxable value and assessed value linked to one-half of the fair market value rather than full market value? Originally, government officials decided that assessed valuation for property tax purposes would be set at one-half of the fair market value as a way of tricking property owners into thinking that their property taxes are less. In actuality, it would have been just as easy to apply one-half of the applicable millage rates to a true market valuation (rather than one-half thereof). When the property tax system was set up in Michigan, government officials apparently thought that property owners would pay more attention to their assessed valuations (as set at one-half of the value) than the millage rates and somehow believe they are getting a "better deal" regarding property taxes. However, time has proven that property owners are not that naïve.

The property tax assessment and collection process in Michigan appears to have been calculated to place most of the burden and criticism on local officials, while letting other governmental units "off the hook." In Michigan, it is the local unit of government (city, village, or township) and its tax assessor which sets property valuations, applies the millages for all of the taxing units of government, sends out the tax bill (which includes not only the taxes from that local unit of government but also for other units of government such as school districts, counties, the state, libraries, etc.), collects the taxes, and defends the assessments if appealed. Local government must bear the expenses of performing those functions, while receiving little reimbursement for collecting taxes for the other units of government. Thus, while the local unit of government is collecting for all units of government, it also takes most of the criticism for property tax collection.

Chapter 30
"BUT I HAVE DEEDED ACCESS ..."

IT IS NOT ONLY PURCHASERS OF WATERFRONT properties who must be cautious regarding a land purchase. Prospective purchasers of off-water properties that purport to have use or access rights to a nearby lake, river, or other body of water must be just as cautious.

Properties that do not have actual frontage on a body of water (and hence, are not riparian), but are located near the waterfront (often called "backlots"), often have the use of waterfront access devices. Sometimes these devices are "private," whereby the owners of only certain nearby lots or parcels can utilize the lake access device. Such lake access devices can include private road ends at lakes, parallel roads along the shore, easements, walkways, alleys, parks, community beaches, and outlots. Typically, use of those private lake access devices is limited to lot owners within a particular plat or the owners of lots specified in an easement, plat, or similar agreement. Public lake access devices allow any member of the general public to utilize the property involved, but only for the purposes for which the public access device was created or dedicated. Examples of public waterfront access devices include public road ends, alleys, parks, promenades, walkways, and parallel roads along the shore.

No matter what anyone says (whether the seller of the waterfront property involved, a realtor, a local municipal official, or anyone else), if a property does <u>not</u> have actual frontage on a body of water in Michigan, it is not riparian. See *Thompson v Enz*, 379 Mich 667; 154 NW2d 473 (1967); *Thies v Howland*, 424 Mich 282; 380 NW2d 463 (1985). All other properties located close to bodies of water are backlots, and any access rights they might have to the body of water (whether via a private or public lake access device) does not make them riparian.

<u>Most waterfront access devices are very limited.</u> In almost all cases, private lake access devices benefiting certain backlots do not accord any individual backlot exclusive use. In most cases, the backlot property owner shares the lake access device with many other backlot (and potentially, even riparian) property owners. By definition, a public lake access device is not exclusive, and any member of the general public can use the lake access, even if the person involved does not own any property within a 100-mile radius of the body of water.

Unfortunately for backlot property owners, the use of lake access devices under Michigan law is generally severely limited. Although many backlot owners assume that they can install their own dock, permanently moor a boat, lounge, sunbathe, and engage in other typically riparian uses at their nearby lake or river access site, that is generally not the case. Many backlot property owners are bitterly disappointed when they assume that their usage rights as to a waterfront access device are broad, only to find out later after they have purchased their backlot that their lake usage rights are severely limited. Please see Chapter 33 for a more in-depth discussion of water access devices.

Prospective purchasers of any backlot property must also be careful not to be taken in by potentially mistaken or misleading language involving water access devices. For example, the sellers of waterfront properties (as well as sometimes, realtors and advertising materials) frequently indicate that a backlot has "deeded access" to a particular body of water. It is often debatable whether or not the phrase "deeded access" is legally correct or misleading. The phrase is probably technically correct if the backlot in question has a specific water access easement in its recorded chain of title. Even in that situation, however, the phrase "with deeded access" is probably misleading as it implies that the particular backlot has exclusive use of the lake access easement or device, which is normally not the case. When the phrase "with deeded access" is used in conjunction with a lake access device such as a plat-created road end, walkway, alley, park, or similar item, the phrase is probably technically both incorrect and potentially misleading. With such a plat dedicated (and created) lake access device, it strictly does not show up within the chain of title for a particular backlot, nor does the backlot owner have exclusive use of those lake access devices. In most cases, the phrase "with deeded access" is a loaded term that essentially means the ability to use lake access devices with severe use limitations in common with other backlot property owners (and in some cases, along with everyone in the general public!). Accordingly, it is very important for prospective purchasers of a backlot property to do their own due diligence with regard to what water access rights, if any, are potentially available for the backlot they are considering purchasing.

Chapter 31
THE PROFESSIONALS— REALTORS, REAL ESTATE AGENTS, LAWYERS, SURVEYORS, AND OTHERS

THE SALE AND PURCHASE OF A WATERFRONT property often involves various professionals, which can include a realtor, real estate agent, real estate broker, lawyer, surveyor, engineer, and potentially other professionals. Of course, not all or even most of those professionals are necessary for every waterfront real estate transaction. In some cases, however, some or many of those professionals may be involved.

In Michigan, there are generally two types of individuals or brokers who represent buyers or sellers as "agents" regarding the sale of waterfront properties. A realtor is a real estate professional who is a member of the National Association of Realtors. All realtors are real estate agents, but not all real estate agents are realtors. The word "realtor" indicates that the individual has had to meet certain standards in order to be deemed a realtor. A real estate agent has not attained the level of realtor, but is a person who helps sell or lease out real estate, acting as an agent for the property owner or prospective purchaser. A real estate agent is also sometimes referred to as a "real estate broker." A real estate agent is a salesperson regarding real property. Both realtors and real estate agents are sometimes called "brokers" by lay people. Typically, a realtor or real estate agent represents either a buyer or a seller with regard to a particular piece of property, but not both. Realtors and real estate agents are usually compensated via a broker's commission, which is a percentage of the purchase price paid at closing. Such broker fees are theoretically subject to negotiation.

In most areas of Michigan, a broker commission for a residential property is between 4 1/2% and 7% of the purchase price, with 6% or 7% being most common. For vacant waterfront properties, the broker's commission typically ranges between 3% and 7% of the purchase price.

A realtor or real estate agent representing a seller enters into a broker agreement with the seller which is often referred to as a "listing agreement." Where a realtor or real estate agent is representing a buyer, the parties enter into a contract often called a "buyer broker agreement." It is also important for the purchase/sales agreement for a particular piece of property to indicate expressly how the realtor(s) and/or real estate agent(s) will be compensated out of the sales proceeds. If each side is represented by a realtor and/or real estate agent, there is typically language in the purchase/sales agreement indicating that the total broker fees will not exceed a certain percentage of the purchase price and that the two real estate professionals will split the total broker fee equally.

Michigan law requires realtors and real estate agents who are acting as agents of sellers or buyers of real property to advise the potential buyers or sellers with whom they work of the nature of their agency relationship. The most common agency relationships are as follows:

- Seller's agent (the most common form of agency with regard to real property)
- Buyer's agent
- Dual agent
- Transaction coordinator
- Designated agency

Does a buyer or seller of waterfront property really need to engage the services of a realtor or real estate agent? There is no legal requirement that they do so. Nevertheless, most people (particularly sellers of land) do utilize such real estate professionals in Michigan. Why? There are many reasons, including the following:

- Such professionals are usually very knowledgeable about real estate transactions.

- Given their databases, experience, and various techniques, they can help match sellers to buyers and buyers to particular pieces or types of property.

- Use of the multiple listing service.

- Help with providing and filling out important forms such as the purchase/sales agreement and seller disclosure statement.

- They can help guide a buyer or seller through what can be a high anxiety or bewildering process.

- Sometimes, properties need updating (new paint, carpeting, etc.), and real estate professionals can advise sellers about modifications that can help sell the property.

- They can help set realistic sales or purchase prices.

- They can help inform buyers about particular neighborhoods, lakes, or areas.

Utilizing a realtor or real estate agent is particularly helpful given their access to the multiple listing service ("MLS"). MLS allows the agents for both sellers and buyers to search a large database of listed properties. Such searches can be by area, property type, price range, and other characteristics. Generally, a seller who attempts to sell property without a realtor or real estate agent cannot have their listing appear "for sale by owner" in the MLS.

If a seller decides not to use a realtor or real estate agent and attempts to sell a waterfront property by himself/herself, there are a variety of pitfalls potentially involved. In that case, the seller should almost certainly use a real estate attorney to assist the seller with the purchase/sales agreement, closing, and other matters. Although the person could theoretically save money on real estate agent fees by not using a realtor or real estate agent (and there are situations where a buyer will not purchase a property unless the seller assists with paying the broker fee of the buyer's agent), any potential savings could be cut into by the fee of the real estate attorney involved. This certainly is not meant to imply that a buyer or seller should or should not utilize a realtor or real estate agent, or that they should not utilize an attorney even if a realtor or real estate agent is involved. However, following are some of the issues that a potential seller or purchaser of waterfront property should carefully consider with regard to utilizing a realtor, real estate agent, and/or attorney.

If a seller decides to forgo the services of a realtor or real estate agent, the seller may have a difficult time ascertaining a reasonable sales price, as well as being able to successfully seek out potential purchasers given the lack of access to databases freely available to realtors and real estate agents. The seller may have to pay to have an appraisal of the property done to ascertain a realistic sales price (which a realtor or real estate agent would typically already know).

How does a person go about choosing a good realtor or real estate agent? Check out the following:

- Obtain and contact references.
- Ask to see the person's credentials.
- Ask around about the person's reputation.
- Surf the Internet for information about the person.
- Check with the local association of realtors to see if any complaints have been filed against the person or if there has been any disciplinary action.
- Check with state licensing authorities about the person.

Where waterfront property is involved, it is also important to choose a realtor or real estate agent who is knowledgeable about waterfront property.

Should a prospective seller or purchaser of waterfront property utilize their own attorney? If a buyer or seller does not engage the services of a realtor or real estate agent, almost certainly they should retain a good real estate attorney. Even if a seller or buyer uses a realtor or real estate agent, they should seriously consider also engaging the services of an experienced real estate attorney for the transaction. While the presence of modern title insurance commitments and title insurance minimizes the need for the services of an attorney somewhat, there is still a variety of potentially negative issues that can arise with regard to the sale or purchase of waterfront property, such that it is normally prudent to engage one's own real estate attorney (*i.e.,* someone looking out for your best interests). And, the seller or the prospective purchaser may be pleasantly surprised how reasonable the fees of an experienced real estate attorney can be with regard to waterfront property closings. Typically, attorneys need not be involved in depth in such transactions. Sometimes, their services can be limited to a careful review of the purchase/sales agreement (and potential negotiations over its terms) before each party signs the agreement, as well as reviewing the closing documents before closing (including examining title issues) and dealing with any preclosing issues. It is absolutely appropriate for someone who wishes to engage the services of a real estate attorney to ask the attorney ahead of time for a fee estimate or range. Although some sellers, realtors, and real estate agents view such attorney involvement as a potential "deal killer," the overwhelming majority of attorneys try to facilitate such transactions and most realtors and real estate agents welcome the involvement of an experienced real estate attorney.

When a prospective buyer or purchaser is pondering whether to engage the services of a realtor, real estate agent, and/or attorney, they should remember not only how expensive or valuable that the waterfront property involved is, but also the many practical and legal pitfalls which are often associated with such a property.

For example, as discussed earlier, one should never buy waterfront property without having a full survey done before closing. And, quite often, it is prudent to put an express contingency clause in the purchase/sales agreement indicating that a new survey will be done prior to closing and that the buyer need not proceed with the closing (and can cancel the purchase/ sales agreement) if the survey shows any encroachments or the purchaser is not satisfied with the survey results. What issues or problems can a good survey potentially show? There are many, including the following:

- Exact boundary line locations.
- The encroachment of a house, structure, fence, etc., from the adjoining property.
- An encroachment of a house, structure, fence, etc., belonging to the property to be purchased onto the adjoining property.
- The presence of an easement or right-of-way.
- The true size, width, and depth of the property.
- The shape of the property.
- On some surveys, how far the house, accessory building, or other items are from all property lines or the body of water.

- If a private road or access easement to the property is involved, the location and characteristics of that easement.

- If the property fronts on a public road, where the edge of the public road right-of-way is located.

- The legal description for the property (which can often be quite long or intricate).

- The amount of water frontage.

Sometimes, a prospective buyer of a waterfront property will also need to engage the services of a professional inspector, termite specialist, or engineer before closing to determine the property's suitability. Those professionals are discussed in other chapters of this book.

Chapter 32
BROKER AND LISTING AGREEMENTS

WHERE A SELLER LISTS A PROPERTY FOR SALE through a realtor or real estate agent, the seller is first required to sign a listing agreement. That agreement will indicate the terms and conditions of the seller-broker relationship. Typically, the listing agreement will also specify the fee of the realtor or real estate agent, usually expressed as a percentage of the actual price paid for the property at closing. Although broker fees are theoretically negotiable, in Michigan, it is quite common for broker fees on properties with dwellings to be in the 7% range, while vacant land can range from 5% to 10% of the actual sales price.

Most listing agreements state that if a broker provides a willing buyer to the seller on the terms that are offered by the seller and the seller refuses to consummate the agreement, then the broker still obtains his/her fee. Furthermore, most listing agreements are not only exclusive, but also provide that even if a purchaser comes to the transaction entirely apart from the efforts of the broker, the broker still must be paid the real estate commission or broker's fees. Additionally, real estate listing agreements typically provide that the broker will still be due his/her fee for some time period after the listing agreement expires if the property sells later (for example, within six months). Therefore, if a seller has shown the property to a prospective purchaser before the listing agreement has been signed and wants to keep open the option of selling to that prospective purchaser later without paying a broker commission, even though there is a listing agreement, the seller should attempt to negotiate a provision in the listing agreement that no broker fee (or a reduced broker fee) will have to be paid if that specific person ultimately purchases the property.

Chapter 33
LAKE ACCESS DEVICES
AND AREAS

RIPARIAN PROPERTY OWNERS GENERALLY DO NOT, of course, need to utilize any other access sites to reach a body of water (apart, perhaps, from a public boat ramp or lake or river association boat launch to put in and take out large boats) as, by definition, such landowners already have frontage on the body of water involved. However, members of the public and backlot property owners need to use public or private properties or water access devices to gain access to a body of water. Such access points can be either public or private.

As discussed elsewhere in this publication, the owner of a property that does not have actual frontage on a body of water and who must use a lake access site to get to the water is not riparian, no matter how much such owner believes and asserts that he/she is a riparian. Even for those lake access easements that expressly grant backlot property owners broad access and use rights to a body of water that almost approach the actual usage rights of riparians, the backlot property owners involved still are not riparians.

Lake access devices are a difficult topic to summarize, as an entire separate book could be written regarding their nature, status, idiosyncrasies, limitations, and other characteristics. The general types of lake access devices include road ends, roads that "parallel" the shoreline of a body of water, parks, walks or walkways, alleys, promenades, community beaches, and access easements. Where a lake access device has been properly created by plat dedication, a recorded document (such as the reservation of an easement in a deed) or other means, the lake access device (and any rights of usage thereof) still normally exists, even if the adjoining property owners are unaware of its existence and even if it has not been physically improved or generally utilized.

Most lake access devices are created via plat dedication. What is that? Creating a plat or a formal subdivision was a very popular method of developing properties around lakes and other bodies of water in Michigan for almost a century and a half, until a decade or two ago. Plats have been utilized less frequently for new developments recently due to the time-consuming and difficult process that a developer must endure to have a plat approved today. Many new residential developments at or near lakes today involve the site condominium form of development. In many respects, a site condominium development is very similar to a plat.

Throughout Michigan's history, there have been various platting statutes which allow the developer or "proprietor" of a plat to create and "dedicate" certain commonly-used elements or properties to a particular use. Once a property is so dedicated and the plat is approved and recorded, the developer cannot "take back" the dedication; rather, the dedicated properties become permanent, thus according the rights for which they were dedicated to either members of the public or property owners within the plat. If a road, park, alley, walk, or other item in a plat is dedicated "to the use of the public," any member of the general public can use the dedicated item. If the dedicated item is dedicated "to the use of the lot owners" (or similar language), that means that only lot owners within the plat (and potentially, their families and invitees) can use the dedicated item.

Generally, a dedicated item does not constitute a separate property that is owned jointly by the lot owners together or by the public (actually with a public dedication, it would be the local road commission and potentially the local municipality), even though those items are normally shown as separate parcels or properties on the original plat. In most cases, the lot owners or public only have an easement right to use the area in common, with the adjoining lot owners actually owning the land under the dedicated item to the center of that item. It is important to note, however, that such easement and ownership issues are a general legal proposition only, and the actual legal status of a particular dedicated item in a specific situation may differ. Furthermore, ownership issues regarding dedicated items are subject to potential change over time by the decisions of the Michigan appellate courts.

Contrary to popular myth, dedicated lake access devices cannot be extinguished, vacated, moved, or transferred to adjoining property owners by deed (even by the local municipality), nonuse, or similar manner. In order to vacate or change a dedicated platted item, an expensive lawsuit must normally be filed in the county circuit court where the property is located and the circuit court judge has limited powers to order the vacation, extinguishment, or modification of the dedicated item involved. See MCL 560.221 *et seq.*

Perhaps the most common lake access device is a road, street, promenade, or alley that ends at or is perpendicular to a lake. These are often referred to as "road ends." Such road ends can either be public (for members of the general public) or private (for lot owners within only the plat involved). In almost all cases, such road ends can be used for ingress, egress, and access only to and from the lake — that is, travel only. See *Jacobs v Lyon Twp (after remand)*, 199 Mich App 667; 502 NW2d 382 (1993), and *Higgins Lake Property Owners Assn v Gerrish Twp*, 255 Mich App 83; 662 NW2d 387 (2003); see also the comprehensive January 30, 2008, formal opinion by the Michigan Attorney General (No. 7211). Generally, such road ends (as well as the shoreline and bottomlands attributable thereto) cannot lawfully be used for the installation and usage of a dock or docks, boat hoists, mooring items, or similar items, nor can they be used for lounging, sunbathing, picnicking, camping, partying, permanent boat mooring, or similar nontravel uses. *Ibid.* Basically, road ends can be used for foot traffic to and from the lake, hand launching small boats, swimming, fishing, and temporary boat mooring (normally, while the owner of the boat is physically present). In some instances, if a public road end is wide enough and the topography is suitable, the local municipality can improve a road end for a public boat ramp or can install one municipal dock for temporary mooring (day use) only. Nevertheless, private docks and boat hoists cannot be used.

The following are cases where the Michigan appellate courts have held that <u>private</u> streets, alleys, walkways, and easements which terminate at a lake (a) generally cannot have any dock, pier or wharf thereon, (b) boats or watercraft cannot be permanently moored, kept, or docked, and (c) lounging, sunbathing, and picnicking cannot occur:

- *Delaney v Pond*, 350 Mich 685; 86 NW2d 816 (1957).

- *Miller v Petersen, et al*, unpublished Michigan Court of Appeals decision issued December 27, 1989 (Docket No. 111358) (10-foot-wide lake access easement).

- *Trustdorf v Benson, et al*, unpublished Michigan Court of Appeals decision issued December 21, 1989 (Docket No. 103109) (25-foot-wide lake access easement).

- *Thies v Howland*, 424 Mich 282; 380 NW2d 463 (1985).

- *Gross v Mills*, unpublished Michigan Court of Appeals decision September 28, 1999; 1999 WL 33435472 (Docket No. 211776) (10-foot-wide lake access easement).

- *Hoisington v Parkes*, unpublished Michigan Court of Appeals decision issued March 12, 1999; 1999 WL 33454008 (Docket No. 204515) (10-foot-wide lake access easement).

- *Dyball v Lennox*, 260 Mich App 698; 680 NW2d 522 (2003) (10-foot-wide lake access easement).

- *Koker v Michaels*, unpublished Michigan Court of Appeals decision issued November 7, 2006; 2006 WL 3208673 (Docket No. 270524) (lake access easement).

- *Pentz v Schlimgen*, unpublished Michigan Court of Appeals decision issued December 19, 2006; 2006 WL 3733236 (Docket No. 258130) (private road and lake access area).

- *Chauvette v Owczarek*, unpublished Michigan Court of Appeals decision issued October 26, 2006; 2006 WL 3039971 (Docket No. 262473) (private road that terminates at Mullett Lake).

- *Gee v Howard*, unpublished Michigan Court of Appeals decision issued November 9, 2006; 2006 WL 3246463 (Docket No. 269732) (several private roadways ending at Lake Lansing).

- *City of Novi v Evers*, unpublished Michigan Court of Appeals decision issued May 6, 2010 (Docket No. 290079) (narrow lake access easement).

- *John Guidobono II Revocable Trust v Jones*, unpublished Michigan Court of Appeals decision issued June 24, 2010 (Docket No. 290589) (lake access easement).

- *Sullivan v Tillman*, unpublished Michigan Court of Appeals decision dated June 2, 2009 (Docket No. 285195) (walk and "beach").

In addition to the above-mentioned appellate cases involving <u>private</u> roads and easements that terminate at Michigan lakes, there is also significant case law in Michigan regarding <u>public</u> roads and easements that terminate at lakes. And, in fact, the case law in Michigan regarding public ways terminating at lakes is very similar to that involving private ways that terminate at lakes. The only significant distinction is that the courts are less likely to allow a dock for temporary boat mooring at a private road end or easement than where a public road or easement terminates at a lake. Some of the significant Michigan appellate decisions involving <u>public</u> roads or easements that terminate at lakes are as follows:

- *Jacobs v Lyon Twp* (after remand), 199 Mich App 667; 502 NW2d 382 (1993).
- *Higgins Lake Property Owners Assn v Gerrish Twp*, 255 Mich App 83; 662 NW2d 387 (2003).
- *Higgins Lake Shores Lakefront Property Owners v Lyon Twp*, Michigan Court of Appeals decision issued December 2, 2008; 2008 WL 5076595 (Docket No. 278894).
- *Magician Lake Homeowners Assn, Inc v Keller Twp Bd of Trustees*, Michigan Court of Appeals decision issued July 31, 2008; 2008 WL 2938650 (Docket No. 278469).
- *Higgins Lake Property Owners Assn v Gerrish Twp*, Michigan Court of Appeals decision issued October 20, 2005; 2005 WL 2727702 (Docket Nos. 262494, 262533, and 262717).
- *Kleiner v Wachowicz*, Michigan Court of Appeals decision issued February 12, 2004; 2004 WL 258259 (Docket Nos. 244053, 244328).
- *Douglas v Harting*, Michigan Court of Appeals decision issued December 18, 2008; 2008 WL 5273425 (Docket No. 277892).

When dealing with a relatively narrow plat-dedicated walk, alley, or similar item that ends at a body of water, whether public or private, the Michigan courts have generally held that those lake access devices are also for travel only. Sedentary uses such as permanent boat mooring, lounging, sunbathing, swimming, private dockage, private boat lifts, etc., are prohibited. See *Thies v Howland*, 424 Mich 282; 380 NW2d 463 (1985). Normally, such public lake access devices are so narrow that even a municipal dock or temporary boat mooring are typically not permitted.

In a few plats, properties on a body of water have been dedicated as a park or beach. Again, those items can be publicly or privately dedicated. The Michigan appellate case law regarding these lake access devices is less well developed. Nevertheless, the Michigan appellate courts have generally held that parks and beaches can be used for lounging, sunbathing, picnicking, swimming, and fishing. See *Dobie v Morrison*, 227 Mich App 536; 575 NW2d 817 (1998). In most cases, dockage, permanent boat mooring (*i.e.,* overnight or when the owner of the boat is not present), boat hoist use, and similar uses cannot occur. See *Turner v Zimmerman*, unpublished Michigan Court of Appeals decision issued May 1, 2007 (Docket Nos. 265008 and 265013); *Magician Lake Homeowners Assn, Inc v Keller Twp Bd of Trustees*, unpublished Michigan Court of Appeals decision issued July 31, 2008; 2008 WL 2938650 (Docket No. 278469) (parks and beaches). However, courts in a relatively few cases have allowed limited permanent boat mooring and dockage if such uses have been present for a long period of time and occurred at the time the park or beach was created. See *Dobie v Morrison*, 227 Mich App 536; 575 NW2d 817 (1998). With a public park, the municipality can probably install one or more public docks, but they normally must be for temporary or day use only.

In many plats in Michigan, a dedicated public road runs along the shore of a body of water, where there was no intervening land between the public road right-of-way and the lake when the plat was created. These are so-called "parallel roads." In the past, the Michigan appellate courts have held that parallel roads could not be used for the general public for dockage, boat moorage, etc. See *McCardel v Smolen*, 71 Mich App 560; 250 NW2d 496 (1976), reversed on other grounds, 404 Mich 89; 273 NW2d 3 (1978); *Croucher v Wooster*, 271 Mich 337; 260 NW 739 (1935). The first tier lot owners are deemed to be riparian, with their side lot lines extending under and through the public road right-of-way to the lake. Such riparian property owners have full dockage, boat moorage, and other riparian rights, subject only to the public's use of the road right-of-way for road purposes only. *2000 Baum Family Trust v Babel*, 488 Mich 136; 793 NW2d 633 (2010).

Not all lake access devices are platted (dedicated) property items. It is also very common for lake access easements to be created across one or more lakefront properties for the benefit of certain backlot properties. Typically, these are created by an express grant or reservation in a deed or other instrument, where a landowner owns both lakefront and offlake properties and wishes to increase the value and marketability of backlot properties by creating or reserving lake access easements for those offlake properties when they are sold. Nevertheless, such lake access easements can also be created via prescriptive easement (similar to "squatter's rights," based on longstanding usage by backlot property owners), by mutual agreement in a recorded document, and similar documents. Such easements only benefit the offlake properties expressly mentioned in the document creating the easement. The overwhelming majority of lake access easements are also for travel purposes only; that is, no dockage, permanent boat moorage, anchoring, storing, or boat hoist use, and no lounging, sunbathing, picnicking, etc. See *Delaney v Pond*, 350 Mich 685; 86 NW2d 816 (1957). That is true whenever the language creating an easement simply mentions an easement, or words of travel such as ingress, egress, access, use of, and to/from. However, in a few cases, easements on their face expressly create broad water usage rights for backlot property owners in situations where a document creating the easement expressly mentions docks, dockage rights, boat mooring, riparian use, or similar language. See *Little v Kin*, 249 Mich App 502; 644 NW2d 375 (2002); partially reversed on other grounds; 468 Mich 699; 664 NW2d 749 (2003).

Many purchasers of backlot properties make the mistake of assuming that a lake access easement benefiting the backlot or a nearby road end, alley, walk, or park at the lake will allow that person to use the lakefront device as their own and that they will be able to install a dock, moor one or more boats there all summer season, and generally lounge, sunbathe, and picnic. And, in almost all such cases, the backlot owners will eventually be proven wrong and will likely be bitterly disappointed. <u>Lake access usually means access (travel) only!</u>

A prospective purchaser of a backlot might wonder what good is a lake access device if the purchaser cannot install or utilize a dock, have one or more boat slips, or lounge or sunbathe at the lake access device. And it is true that the uses a person can make of such a lake access device is generally very limited. Nevertheless, even with limited usage lake access devices, backlot property owners generally have the right to walk to and from the water, swim, fish, ice fish in the winter, utilize a snowmobile in the winter, temporarily moor a boat (for example, when picking someone up or dropping someone off), and similar uses. Even such limited lake access rights can prove valuable and should not be belittled.

What about a situation where a backlot property owner was led to believe (before purchasing the backlot property) that he or she would be able to utilize a particular lake access device for permanent boat moorage, lounging, and sunbathing, and that later proves not to be the case? In almost no situation will a promise or representation by the seller, realtor or real estate agent, neighbor, or other person enable the buyer of the backlot to lawfully violate the usage limitations of a particular lake access device. In some cases, the buyer might have a legal cause of action for damages against a seller, realtor, or real estate agent who misrepresented the allowable usage rights to a lake access device. And, in a few rare cases, the backlot owner might have a claim based upon the prescriptive easement doctrine to permanently engage in certain additional uses and activities at the lake access device, but such rights must be vindicated in court first and are often expensive and difficult to establish. It is clear that backlot property owners who are potentially relying on a lake access device for water access should carefully consider all of the pitfalls prior to purchasing a backlot property near a body of water.

What about prospective purchasers of true waterfront property—need they worry about lake access devices? Researching lake access devices on, adjacent to, or near the lakefront property they are considering purchasing is very important. On occasion, a lake access device (such as an easement) will actually be located on (and encumber) a lakefront lot or property. In most situations, such lake access device will show up on the title insurance commitment if it is located (wholly or partially) on the lot or property to be purchased. In most cases, if it is located on the parcel or lot to be purchased, the lake access device will be an easement. In a few cases, a prescriptive easement could exist on the waterfront parcel or lot that does not show up in the title insurance commitment. In either case, having any type of lake access easement located on the parcel or lot being purchased could have a devastating impact upon the value of that property, as well as the potential use and enjoyment of any prospective purchaser. Almost as troublesome to a new owner of a waterfront parcel is a lake access device located adjacent to, or adjoining, that lakefront property (which will usually not show up on a title search or title insurance commitment). Many waterfront property owners who have a public or private road end, easement, alley, walk, or similar lake access device located adjacent to their property have experienced terrible headaches based on trespass, encroachments, loud parties, "incidents" involving personal conflict, and similar unpleasant situations. Accordingly, a prospective purchaser should buy a waterfront property with a lake access device located thereon or adjacent thereto only if the purchaser has fully done his/her due diligence and is willing to live with the situation. In cases where members of the public or backlot property owners are misusing a lake access device, an adjoining or nearby riparian property owner normally cannot rely upon state, county, or local municipal officials to assist (they consider such problems to be private civil matters), but must often resort to expensive litigation.

Chapter 34
EASEMENTS

AN EASEMENT IS THE PERMANENT RIGHT TO USE A portion of the property of another for a specific use or purpose. Easements are typically created (or reserved) by an express document, whether it be a deed, land contract, dedication in a plat, a deed restriction document, or a specific easement agreement. In order to be valid, "run with the land," and to bind and benefit future property owners, easements must be in writing and recorded with the county register of deeds. One exception to this rule is a prescriptive easement (see Chapter 17).

The majority of easements are rights of travel across the property of another. These can include easements for private roads, walkways, stairs, alleys, and similar items. In fact, most public road rights-of-way are glorified easements. Although most easements are for travel purposes, other easements do exist for other uses. Those nontravel uses that can be authorized by easement include parking, utilities, dockage and boat moorage, septic drain fields, drainage, wells, and storage. The common land preservation device referred to as a "conservation easement" is actually a misnomer; a conservation easement is really a deed restriction or restrictive covenant (preventing development and certain other uses), not a true easement.

A prospective purchaser of a property should be aware
that there may be both easements benefiting that property as
well as burdening the property. Some of the easements that can
benefit a particular property (often referred to as an easement
"appurtenant," which means that it benefits the property and is
"attached to" that property[26]) include private road and private
utility easements across the adjoining properties of others.
Easements that can potentially bind and be located on a property to
be purchased (that may also benefit other properties) also include
segments of a private road easement, utility easements, walkway
easements, drainage easements, and well or septic easements.

All other matters being equal, it is best not to purchase a
property that has one or more easements running across (and
binding) that property.[27] Why? Easements are encumbrances.
Easements across a property can often "cloud title." Having
easements located on one's property can cause the landowner
to lose control of significant aspects of the property. That is
particularly true of access or private road easements for other
properties that can make a property owner whose land is subject to
such an easement feel like he or she does not own a chunk of their
own property.

Some easements are "dormant." That is, they still exist, but
have not been used or developed (or at least not for many years).
Unfortunately, some purchasers of property bound by dormant
easements assume that over a period of time, the easement
will become invalid or that the easement will never be utilized
for the purpose for which it is granted. Both assumptions can
prove frustratingly wrong. Almost never can an easement be
extinguished or lost by abandonment or mere nonuse. Likewise,
an easement that has lain dormant for decades (or longer) can
suddenly be developed by the beneficiary or beneficiaries of the
easement for the purposes allowed. All of a sudden, that unused
private road easement on your property that serves another parcel,
an unused and undeveloped stairway easement across your land
to the beach, or an unused drainage easement on your property
may be improved and utilized. Quite often, an easement benefits
not only one property but several or many adjoining or nearby
properties.

For lakefront property owners, among the most frustrating
easements can be easements in the form of plat dedications (or the
equivalent) located between the shore and the lakefront property or

along the edge of a lakefront property (going to the body of water) for use as a park, private or public road, alley, walkway, or beach. Please also see Chapter 33.

Of course, some easements are really no big deal. For example, most properties have a utility easement located along the nonwaterfront edge of their property. Every property that borders a public road right-of-way has a significant portion of the undeveloped portion of the road right-of-way extending 10, 20, 30, or even more feet into their property. Quite often, drainage easements on one's land are not a problem (although in some case, they can be trouble).

Easements are items not to be trifled with.

Footnotes

[26] Other easements do not benefit a particular property and are called "easements in gross" (for example, public road easements and public utility easements).

[27] There are, of course, exceptions to this. Private road easements benefiting the lot or parcel involved and utility easements that do not interfere with the property's use are examples of acceptable easements on one's land.

Chapter 35
WARRANTIES, GUARANTEES, AND THE LIKE

THE PURCHASE OF LAKEFRONT PROPERTY TRULY invokes the old phrase, "buyer beware (*caveat emptor*)." That is normally true not only with regard to any cottage or dwelling located on the waterfront property, but also with regard to the land itself and associated bottomlands.

In Michigan, there is no common law or statutory warranty for used homes, dwellings, or cabins. Furthermore, the standard purchase/sales agreement usually contains an "as-is" clause, which means that the purchaser typically takes the property (including the dwelling and the physical aspects of the land itself) without any kind of guarantee or warranty (except perhaps as to title). Of course, the seller can voluntarily grant a warranty for a dwelling with express language in the purchase/sales agreement or other contractual document. That is most common in the context of a builder who owns a lakefront property, builds a dwelling thereon, and sells the property with the new dwelling to a third party with an express warranty. However, even where an express warranty is given in writing, it is subject to any limitations contained in the warranty language. Furthermore, the financial wherewithal behind the warranty is only as good as the person or entity giving the warranty.

Utilizing an "as-is" clause does not completely insulate a seller from liability under all circumstances. If the seller (or the seller's agent) makes express representations or promises regarding the condition of a dwelling (or matters related thereto), a seller could potentially be liable for fraud or otherwise, notwithstanding the lack of a common law or statutory warranty or the presence of an as-is clause. Furthermore, if the seller omits or misrepresents material matters in the Seller's Disclosure Form (required by MCL 565.951), that could also cause the seller to incur liability to the property purchaser.

Is there such a thing as "silent fraud" in Michigan? Yes. Silent fraud involves a situation where the seller is aware of and fails to disclose a significant problem or defect. While the seller may not actively misrepresent the matter, the seller engages in some type of representation by words or actions that is false or misleading and is intended to deceive, *i.e.,* fraudulent concealment. *Roberts v Saffell,* 280 Mich App 397, 404; 760 NW2d 715 (2008). Generally speaking, "as is" clauses will not transfer the risk of loss to the buyer where the seller engages in fraud before the purchase/sales agreement is signed.

The land comprising a waterfront property normally does not have any warranty at all, except for the title warranty contained in a warranty deed. With regard to the physical aspects of waterfront property, however, the buyer clearly proceeds at his or her own risk. Waterfront properties are not warranted or guaranteed to be "buildable," free of wetlands, sinkholes, shifting earth or fill, have good bottomlands, or similar matters. That is why it is so important for the purchaser to place the appropriate inspection clauses in the purchase/sales agreement and to do a thorough job in inspecting and checking out the real property itself during the due diligence period between the date on which the purchase/sales agreement is signed and the date of closing.

Chapter 36
LEGAL REMEDIES, A BREAKDOWN IN PARTY RELATIONSHIPS, AND LITIGATION

GENERALLY, LITIGATION RELATED TO REAL ESTATE transactions is to be avoided at all costs. Litigation is not only time consuming and expensive, but the results are almost always unpredictable. Sometimes, where a party has a "surefire winner" going into court, a judge or jury surprises everyone and rules against that party. Furthermore, there are occasions where one party to a lawsuit has an exceedingly weak position, but still prevails in court.

Attorney fees and costs in litigation can be very high. Furthermore, Michigan follows the so-called "American system" of attorney fees, whereby each party normally pays their own attorney fees without reimbursement from the other party, win, lose, or draw. Most other industrialized nations in the world utilize the "English system" of attorney fees, whereby the loser in court pays some or all of the attorney fees of the winner.

What should one do if the other party to a real estate transaction breaches the purchase/sales agreement, refuses to close, or engages in other wrongful conduct? Unfortunately, some situations leave a party no choice but to pursue litigation. However, prior to filing a lawsuit, all other avenues should be exhausted. Sometimes, simply involving an attorney can resolve the matter. If that does not work, every community in Michigan has some type of mediation or arbitration services available, whereby the parties to a real estate transaction can utilize an objective third party (or parties) to help resolve the dispute. Mediation is a process whereby the neutral mediator or mediators try to help the parties reach a negotiated compromise settlement. The mediators are facilitators and do not make any type of binding final decision regarding the controversy. Arbitration typically involves one third party objective arbitrator who makes a binding decision after a mini-trial.

What are the remedies of the prospective purchaser of a waterfront property if the seller will not close the real estate transaction or attempts to close in violation of the purchase/sales agreement? If the seller engages in a significant breach of contract and the buyer does not want to proceed to closing (for example, the seller cannot provide marketable title or the buyer has appropriately invoked one of the contingencies to get out of the contract by providing the seller with the appropriate notice), the buyer can either sue to obtain back his or her earnest money and to cancel the purchase/sales agreement, or alternately, pursue a lawsuit for specific performance. Specific performance normally involves a lawsuit to force a real estate closing to occur.

What if the prospective purchaser breaches — what are the seller's remedies? In most cases, the seller will sue for specific performance, to force the buyer to proceed with the closing and real estate purchase. If the buyer is obligated to close but is unable to do so, it is also possible that specific performance will not occur but that the seller can obtain damages from the buyer (for example, loss of the damages associated with the failure to close if the seller is only able to sell the real estate later at a loss, and any incidental damages the seller might incur).

How can a buyer or seller best avoid litigation associated with a real estate purchase or sale?

- Use a highly qualified real estate professional or professionals (a realtor, real estate agent, and/or skilled real estate attorney).

- Do not assume anything. Put everything in writing! Not only should the purchase/sales agreement be in writing, but also any side agreements, notices, etc. It is best to follow up all substantive conversations regarding a real estate deal with an email or letter.

- If a deal appears to be too good to be true, it probably is!

- Pursue due diligence with a vengeance!

- Don't sign any purchase/sales agreement until you understand all of its terms and all of the clauses and requirements that you want are clearly contained in the written agreement.

- Don't purchase anything based on emotion.

- Normally, go with your first instincts, unless significant evidence indicates you should do otherwise.

- Don't make snap decisions.

- Reread this book!

Chapter 37
SOME MYTHS ASSOCIATED WITH BUYING AND OWNING WATERFRONT PROPERTY

MANY MYTHS AND MISCONCEPTIONS HAVE ARISEN over the years regarding lakefront properties in Michigan. My favorites include:

1. **Myth:** Members of the public and other riparian property owners can walk around an inland lake without permission so long as they stay in the water or on the shore.

   Fact: Unless there is a public road right-of-way, easement, park, or other encumbrance between the lake and the riparian properties, members of the public and other riparians do not have the right to walk on the lakefront or bottomlands of another at an inland lake without permission. For Great Lakes shorelines, the rule is different. Pursuant to the "beachwalker" case (*Glass v Goeckel*, 473 Mich 667; 703 NW2d 58 (2005)), the public generally has an easement for walking lakeward of the ordinary high water mark.

2. **Myth:** Riparian boundary lines under an inland lake radiate out to the center of the lake in the same direction as the side lot lines of the riparian property on land.

   Fact: That is almost never the case. Riparian boundary lines under the water of an inland lake tend to radiate in a pie-like fashion toward the center of the lake.

3. Myth: Every lake in Michigan has a public access site. Or, another variation of this myth is that every lake in the state of Michigan has a public road end (often called a "section line road") that affords public access to the lake, even if it is not known or is well-hidden.

Fact: That is false. While it is true that many lakes in Michigan have public access sites, including public roads which terminate at the lake and accord limited public access, not every lake in Michigan has such public access points nor is there any requirement that every lake have a public access point or site. It is amazing how often I hear people assert this myth. To date, however, no person reciting this myth has ever been able to show me a statute or any court case which supports this myth.

4. Myth: A local government's jurisdiction ends at the water's edge.

Fact: While a local municipality's jurisdiction beyond the water's edge is questionable on the Great Lakes, with inland lakes, a municipality can have full zoning and other ordinance jurisdiction over all parts of an inland lake. Of course, if the inland lake straddles two or more municipalities, a particular municipality's jurisdiction ends at the portion of the lake where the other municipality's geographical jurisdiction begins.

5. Myth: It is lawful to place large piles of sand on the beach and to occasionally shovel some sand in the water or let the elements wash the sand into the lake, and there is no need for a permit for such sand.

Fact: No sand or fill can occur on any body of water in Michigan lakeward or riverward of the ordinary high water mark without a permit. On inland lakes, the permit must be obtained from the Michigan Department of Natural Resources and the Environment. On the Great Lakes, a permit must be obtained from the U.S. Army Corps of Engineers (and sometimes also from the DNRE). Where an inland lake has a direct navigable passage to one of the Great Lakes, it is possible that a permit will have to be obtained from both agencies. Placing a pile of sand landward of the ordinary high water mark and allowing it to "erode" or wash into a lake or river beyond the ordinary high water mark would likely be a violation of state or federal statute if no permit is obtained for in-water sanding.

6. **Myth:** If I have a lake access easement, I have the right to install a dock, moor a boat, lounge, sunbathe, and picnic.

Fact: As discussed in depth in this book, lake access easements almost never accord the beneficiaries such rights.

7. **Myth:** I do not have to worry too much about the purchase/sales agreement that I will be signing regarding the purchase of a piece of property in Michigan, since many of the details can be worked out later even if not expressly mentioned in the agreement.

Fact: In almost all cases, a signed purchase/sales agreement for real estate in Michigan is a fully binding contract that cannot be varied or supplemented without the express written consent of all parties to the contract.

8. **Myth:** With regard to any zoning, DNRE permit, local ordinance, or other requirements, it is best to simply do the lake project you want to do without a permit and ask for forgiveness/permission later if anyone finds out.

Fact: That is almost never a good move. The penalties for violating a state or federal law or local ordinance regarding the waterfront can be extreme. Furthermore, you might have to "undo" the project at great personal cost.

9. **Myth:** On an inland lake, riparians only own to the edge of the water, such that I can anchor my boat overnight out into the lake anywhere I want.

Fact: With almost all inland lakes in Michigan, the adjoining riparian property owners own the bottomlands adjacent to their lot or parcel to the center of the lake. While boaters and fishermen can temporarily moor or anchor their boat on the bottomlands of another while fishing or recreating, only the riparian landowner has the right to anchor or moor a boat or watercraft on his/her bottomlands permanently or overnight.

10. **Myth:** Since the local municipality has no ordinance regulations regarding docks or swimming rafts, I can extend my dock as far as I want out into the lake or keep my raft in the middle of the lake, so long as it is on my bottomlands, and there is nothing anyone can do about it.

Fact: Unreasonably long docks or raft locations that interfere with navigability are subject to two types of regulation absent a local municipal ordinance. First, pursuant to the Michigan Marine Safety Act, the DNRE has the ability to require that a raft or dock be moved or removed if it interferes with navigability. See MCL 324.80101 *et seq.* Second and alternately, other riparians potentially have a civil remedy against you in court if your dock or raft unreasonably interferes with their riparian rights. See *West Michigan Dock & Market Corp v Lakeland Investments*, 210 Mich App 505; 534 NW2d 212 (1995).

11. **Myth:** In Michigan, a parcel or lot cannot be landlocked or inaccessible.

    Fact: A parcel or lot can be landlocked or inaccessible, legally or practically. Today, most municipalities will not allow a new parcel or lot to be created unless it has frontage on a public road or approved private road. Nevertheless, there are a number of parcels or lots throughout Michigan created years ago that are landlocked or inaccessible and that cannot be made accessible unless an adjoining property owner voluntarily sells or creates an easement. On occasion, the owner of a landlocked parcel or lot can go to court and obtain a permanent access easement via the common law doctrines of prescriptive easement, implied easement, or easement by necessity, but those remedies are not available in all cases.

Chapter 38
LIABILITY AND FLOOD INSURANCE (ONCE YOU BUY THAT WATERFRONT PROPERTY)

AN AMAZING NUMBER OF RIPARIANS ARE underinsured when it comes to liability insurance coverage for their own lake property and activities. Many riparians still have liability insurance coverage of only $300,000 to $500,000 for their lake property. Given that jury verdicts or even settlements in excess of $1,000,000 (or more) are not uncommon, prudence dictates that liability insurance coverage below $1,000,000 (and in many cases, even more) is probably unwise.

Lakefront properties and their appurtenances pose potential injury or death situations not present for conventional dry land properties. For instance, riparian properties carry water risks such as drowning, diving into shallow water from a dock or swimming raft, ice accidents, and similar high-risk situations. Boat propellers, high-speed boating, water skiing, personal watercraft, water trampolines and other water "toys" all increase the risk of injury or even death.

Many property owners believe that they can only be sued if they are, in fact, at fault. Unfortunately, even claims without merit often end up in litigation, such that the property owner will have to legally defend himself/herself. The attorney fees and court costs involved in defending against a tort or damages action alone can exceed $50,000, $100,000 or more, even if one ultimately prevails in court. Furthermore, under the American system of attorney fees, in most cases, each side pays its own attorney fees, regardless of who prevails in court. In addition to the legal defense costs for trial, riparians should also consider the additional attorney fees and costs associated with any appeal (whether by the property owner or the party bringing the lawsuit). Most liability insurance policies cover not only potential damages judgments against the insured, but also typically pay for the legal defense costs including attorney fees (although there are always policy limits). Whether or not a property owner is at fault for the damages, injury, or death involved is a question of fact to be determined by a judge or jury, and the results can often be unpredictable.

Proper and sufficient liability insurance coverage can also give you peace of mind. If one is unfortunate enough to have a damages verdict rendered against them in court for an injury or death occurring at their property and the insurance coverage is not sufficient to cover the damages verdict, the property owner would normally be personally liable for the portion of the verdict not covered by insurance proceeds. In some situations, that can financially ruin a person, prompt bankruptcy, or both.

A common minimum recommended liability insurance amount for residential lake properties in Michigan is $1,000,000, although some experts recommend $1,500,000 or even $2,000,000. Quite often, for homeowners, a liability insurance policy "umbrella" can be purchased on top of the normal homeowners or other liability insurance policy (for example, a $1,000,000 liability insurance umbrella on top of a basic $300,000 liability coverage for the lakefront house). Of course, if you have a teenage driver or drivers in your family, liability insurance premiums can be dramatically higher.

Generally, liability insurance policies for lakefront property will not cover any damages, lawsuits or related matters arising out of the use of a boat, personal watercraft, four-wheeler, snowmobile, or other vehicles—normally, a person must purchase separate policies (or policy riders) for coverage for such vehicles.

Homeowners should also confirm with their insurance agent that their liability insurance policy will cover lake appurtenances such as docks, boat lifts, swim rafts, water trampolines, and similar items. If there is an injury or death at or involved with a lakefront property, the homeowner should notify his/her insurance carrier immediately. That might not only be required by the insurance policy itself, but it is often helpful to have the insurance company potentially investigate the facts and circumstances soon after the accident rather than at some later time when evidence is "stale."

Should you insure your vacant waterfront property? Yes! Even injured trespassers can sue for injuries incurred on vacant properties. Although they might not prevail in court in a given case, the attorney fees and defense costs to the innocent landowner can still be quite high. Sometimes, even vacant lakefront property can be covered by one's homeowners insurance policy.

What is flood insurance? Flood insurance is purchased by the owner of waterfront property (or nonlakefront properties within flood areas) in order to protect the dwelling or accessory buildings on the property. Flood insurance is not mandatory *per se*—there is no law or statute that requires a property owner to purchase flood insurance if there is no applicable financing or other insurance requirements. Nevertheless, purchasing and maintaining flood insurance is frequently a requirement of a bank or lending institution so long as a mortgage or other financing is outstanding regarding a lakefront property or properties in an area subject to flooding. Typically, lenders will order or require a flood insurance certificate prior to closing to establish whether or not the property is within a floodplain or flood zone. Not all lakefront properties require flood insurance for the financing lender—generally, only those in a floodplain or similar area. Unfortunately, in some cases, a lender will require flood insurance even where the dwelling or improvements are located outside of a flood zone or floodplain due to conservative lending practices. A property purchaser (*i.e.*, a borrower) who has good reason to dispute a floodplain, flood zone or flood hazard determination made by a lender may request that the Federal Emergency Management Administration ("FEMA") review that determination; however, that can be a time-consuming process.

Unfortunately, flood insurance can be quite expensive. In certain floodplain areas around Michigan, owners of the lakefront properties in such areas qualify for federally-subsidized flood insurance. Even with federal subsidization, however, premiums for such flood insurance can still be quite high. Prior to purchasing a lakefront property (or property potentially in a flood zone), the prospective purchaser should check to determine whether flood insurance will be required, and if so, how much the premiums will be. Of course, even if flood insurance premiums for a given property are relatively modest today, they could go up substantially in the future.

Chapter 39
TYPES OF LAKES

IN MICHIGAN, THERE ARE, OF COURSE, MANY
different types of lakes. But, does the type of lake involved have
any legal significance?

The biggest distinction involves one of the Great Lakes versus
an inland lake. This distinction has a number of legal implications,
including, but not limited to, bottomlands ownership, the ability to
install a dock or pier, the right of members of the public to walk on
the bottomlands and shoreline, and similar matters.

Quite often, lay people will refer to a "public lake" or a
"private lake." However, there is no overriding definition for
what constitutes a public versus a private lake, nor an overarching
legal distinction between the two types of lakes. In common
vernacular, a public lake usually means a lake with some type of
public access (whether it be a public park, boat launch, road end,
or similar access). When a lake is categorized as being "private,"
that generally means that there is no public access site and a
member of the public cannot lawfully reach the lake unless invited
by a riparian property owner. There are a few statutes that do
differentiate between a public and private lake, but only for one
highly-specialized purpose or reason. See, for example, MCL 41.418
or MCL 324.30902(1) and 324.30904. Contrary to public myth, not
all lakes have (or must have) a public access site, point, or property.

What is the difference between a lake versus a pond? Unfortunately, the Michigan common law has not drawn a bright line to define a pond versus a lake. However, the administrative agencies in Michigan generally consider a pond to be five acres in size or smaller. Ponds do not have riparian rights.

Another distinction involves "artificial" versus "natural" lakes. Artificial lakes can be created by placing a dam along a river, creek, or stream (or other source of water). Artificial lakes can also be created by digging out areas (for example, former gravel pits) where the groundwater is relatively high. Augmentation wells can also be utilized to create artificial lakes or expand natural lakes. In general, artificial lakes do not have riparian rights (see *Persell v Wertz*, 287 Mich App 576 (2010)), although larger artificial bodies of water may have something akin to riparian rights.

Sales promotional materials for waterfront properties often refer to an "all-sports lake." Again, that phrase has no legal definition or significance. Nevertheless, that phrase is frequently used to describe lakes that are large and deep enough to support a wide variety of recreational activities such as swimming, fishing, water skiing, sailing, and high-speed boating, as well as a lack of restrictions against any of those activities. Some lakes have deed restrictions or special government watercraft rules that prohibit boat engines (except for electric motors), high-speed boating, or water skiing, which would preclude those bodies of water from being considered an all-sports lake.

Scientifically, it is good to know the trophic status (nutrient richness) of the lake involved. In Michigan, a lake can be categorized as oligotrophic, mesotrophic, or eutrophic. The classification will indicate whether the lake has "aged" significantly and the lake's overall health.

In summary, lakes are sometimes informally categorized as:

- Public versus private
- All-sports
- No-wake
- No motor (or electric motor only)
- Deed restricted
- Natural versus artificial
- Spring fed
- The trophic status of a lake

Chapter 40
"IF IT IS A DEVELOPMENT, IT'S GUARANTEED, RIGHT?"

MOST WATERFRONT PROPERTIES IN MICHIGAN (except in very rural areas) are located in developments, whether the development is a plat, condominium, or small-scale development created less formally. Many prospective purchasers of waterfront property assume that if the lot, parcel, or condominium unit they are considering purchasing is located within a development or has been "approved" by the local municipality, then the property must be fully lawful, buildable, etc. Unfortunately, that is not always the case.

Local municipalities are not guarantors of new lots, parcels, or condominium units. Many lots and parcels on lakes, rivers, and streams in Michigan were created many years ago, long before local municipal zoning ordinances, platting ordinances, and other local government regulations. Furthermore, due to limited municipal budgets and other factors, local government review of proposed developments, condominium projects, and new lots and parcels is often quite limited. Finally, if the local government makes a mistake in approving a development, lot, parcel, or condominium unit, the local government generally has governmental immunity (*i.e.*, it is not liable for damages) and is not legally responsible for the error.

Developer liability is one of the few areas under Michigan law that has not been well-developed to protect the consumer. Trying to pursue a developer or the seller of a unbuildable, unlawful, or problematic piece of waterfront property is usually difficult. Furthermore, in many cases, the applicable statute of limitations may have already run, thus leaving a disgruntled purchaser without a remedy and potentially in possession of an unbuildable, unusable, or unlawful waterfront property.

"Buyer beware" is fully applicable with regard to the buildability and lawful status of a waterfront property. Accordingly, one of the issues that a prospective purchaser must pursue as part of his/her due diligence between the time when the purchase/sales agreement is signed and closing is to verify that the condominium unit, lot, or parcel at issue is fully lawful (and if the property is vacant or an old cottage is to be torn down and a new one built, fully buildable). In these tough economic times, it is not uncommon to have developments that are not completely finished (or which have extensive liens, unfulfilled local government requirements, or other problems), whereby a developer has simply walked away. An unsuspecting third-party purchaser might not initially be aware of these problems.

Some of the problems that can be associated with a lot, parcel, or condominium unit in a development, condominium, or less formal development can include the following:

- Some have substandard or even no legal means of access.
- The seller does not have clear title.
- Certain common elements of the development (such as private roads, sewer and water installation, and other utilities) must be completed before the local municipality will allow a lot or parcel to be built on, and such improvements have not been completed. Also, who pays for their completion?
- A seller has effectuated a land division without the proper local municipal approval, and one or more of the resulting parcels or lots are illegal and unbuildable.
- The building site is subject to flooding due to inadequate stormwater facilities or structures.
- The developer or seller of the property has forgotten to provide appropriate utilities or easements to extend electric, natural gas, etc., to the lot or property, or a purchaser assumes that such utilities can be extended or are available and that is not the case.

- As part of the purchase/sales agreement, the developer agrees to construct or finish a dwelling, but is in financial difficulty, thus leaving the purchaser with severe problems in completing the dwelling and clearing all liens, mortgages, encumbrances, etc.

Chapter 41
HELPFUL TIPS FOR THE SELLERS OF WATERFRONT PROPERTY

POTENTIAL BUYERS OF WATERFRONT PROPERTY ARE not the only ones who face a sometimes daunting task, particularly with regard to "due diligence" investigations. Sellers of waterfront property must also be very careful.

Perhaps the best advice that can be given to someone contemplating the sale of a waterfront property is not to exaggerate or misrepresent any of the characteristics of the property. Should that occur, in many cases, it will come back to "bite" you, either in the form of a lawsuit or a bitter purchaser (or both!). For example, if the property involved is a backlot with a shared lake access site, do not advertise or indicate that the property has "deeded access," riparian rights, or similar misrepresentation. Use fully truthful language. Full disclosure (within reason) regarding any problems or "issues" associated with the property is normally the best avenue.

If "deeded access" is normally not a legally-appropriate phrase, what language should the seller of a backlot property near the water use to indicate that a nearby lake access is available? Perhaps the best wording is simply to indicate that "limited lake access to Marble Lake is located nearby." Any language that states or implies that the particular backlot has its own exclusive lake access device, that the backlot has permanent docking and boat mooring privileges, or that the backlot has a lake access device where virtually any use can occur thereon, can get a seller (and potentially, a realtor or real estate agent) in trouble if the wording is not true or accurate. This is one area where exaggeration (or what the seller might consider "puffery") can get a person into trouble.

Prospective buyers are not the only ones who have to be careful regarding the language of the negotiated purchase/sales agreement—sellers must be equally cautious. If there are too many contingencies contained in the written agreement in favor of the buyer, it will make it easier for the buyer to back out of the closing without penalty.

Sellers should make sure that any contract for the sale of their waterfront property contains the appropriate "**As-Is**" language that makes it clear to the prospective purchaser that there are no warranties, guarantees, representations, promises, etc., being made with regard to the waterfront property except, perhaps, the warranties of title to be given in the warranty deed or land contract. A good real estate attorney can assist the seller of a waterfront property with the appropriate language to limit the seller's liability exposure should the purchaser discover something that he/she does not like about the property after closing.

Given all the "toys" associated with most waterfront properties, it is also very important for the seller (as well as the buyer) to specify in the purchase/sales agreement exactly what specific outdoor items are included within the sale and sales price. The contract should address such items as dock sections, swim rafts, boat hoists, lawn furniture, boats, sheds, and any other waterfront paraphernalia. With regard to the interior of the house, movable or removable items such as a washer, dryer, freezer, refrigerator, water softener, trash compactor, and similar items should also be specifically addressed in the purchase/sales agreement.[28]

The seller's realtor or real estate agent can assist the seller with setting a proposed (and realistic) sales price for the waterfront property involved. If the seller wants to get a second opinion regarding the price the property should be listed for, the seller can retain a third-party real estate appraiser to give a more in-depth analysis of the true fair market value of the waterfront property.

If the seller will be retaining ownership of an adjoining lot or parcel after the sale of the land at issue, the seller may want to consider putting one or more recorded deed restrictions or restrictive covenants on the land to be sold (in order to protect the property being kept by the seller). Such restrictions could include prohibitions on mobile homes, further division of the land, setback minimums, a minimum size requirement for any new dwelling, and other restrictions on use. Any such restrictions should be in place before a purchase/sales agreement is signed (or inserted into such an agreement) and drafted by a competent real estate attorney.

While much of the advertising today for the sale of waterfront properties occurs via the Internet, virtual tours, and other techniques in the ethersphere, sellers, realtors, and real estate agents still use temporary outdoor real estate signs fairly extensively for sales. Such signs can be an effective tool for helping to sell real estate. However, it should also be kept in mind that many real estate signs violate not only local municipal sign regulation ordinances, but also potentially the property rights of others.

Almost all local municipalities have sign regulations. For some municipalities, those regulations are found in the municipality's zoning ordinance. In other municipalities, the sign ordinance is a "standalone" ordinance separate from the zoning ordinance. Typically, municipal sign regulations allow one or two outdoor real estate "for sale" signs if installed <u>on the property that is listed for sale</u>. Placing a real estate "for sale" sign on any property other than the property being offered for sale (for example, down the road at a street intersection) is almost always a violation of the local municipal sign regulations. In addition, placing real estate signs on utility poles or installing signs directing prospective buyers to a property located some distance away is almost always unlawful under the local municipality's sign regulations.

Even apart from municipal sign regulations, placing a real estate sign on the property of another without permission is an unlawful trespass. Some sellers are also under the mistaken assumption that it is permissible to place a real estate sign in the public road right-of-way adjacent to another person's property without permission, as the public right-of-way normally extends 10 to 20 feet into the lawn of an adjoining property. However, that too would be a trespass, unless done with the permission of the adjoining property owner. In most cases, the public road right-of-way is akin to an easement to be used for road purposes only and the adjoining property owner still usually owns the land under the public road easement and has the authority to disallow private signs of others without permission.

Finally, placing real estate signs at intersections can be downright dangerous, as such signs can interfere with the clear sight distances necessary for motorist visibility.

All real estate transactions have potential tax (local, state, and federal) consequences, particularly for the seller of real property. Issues regarding income taxes, capital gains, and other taxes relating to a lakefront real estate transaction are beyond the scope of this publication. Nevertheless, sellers and buyers should consult with the appropriate tax professional early on in the property sale or purchase processs.

Footnotes

[28] It is generally also advisable for the parties to execute a "bill of sale" at closing with regard to any non-real estate items that are part of the sale (such as furniture, appliances, docks, swim rafts, etc.). Such a document might be helpful not only for tax purposes, but also for future reference or documentation of the transaction. The seller should also include an "as-is" clause in the bill of sale.

Chapter 42
WHAT THE HECK DOES THAT MEAN? (HELPFUL WATER-FRONT DEFINITIONS)

FOLLOWING ARE THE DEFINITIONS AND MEANINGS of many words, terms, and phrases that arise with regard to waterfront properties in Michigan.

- **Abstract or Abstract of Title:** These are rarely used today. In the past, they were essentially copies of all prior recorded documents regarding the property at issue.

- **Accretion:** The gradual building up or creation of an alluvium (plume) deposit out into the water.

- **Adverse Possession:** The ability to claim adjoining property where the claimant has exclusively used the property of another for 15 years or more. Sometimes also referred to as "squatter's rights."

- **Agency:** This means having a realtor, real estate agent, or the equivalent working for (or representing) you.

- **Assessed Value or Valuation:** This is a Michigan real property tax term. It represents one-half of the fair market value for a piece of real estate for a given year, as determined by the local municipal tax assessor. In actuality, this figure means very little as the actual property tax is based on "taxable value," which is normally less than the assessed valuation. Taxable value is subject to a "cap," which limits the increase in taxable value each year.

- **Avulsion:** A sudden alteration or change regarding a canal or channel. Typically, avulsion does not change boundary lines.

- **Backlot:** A property that does not have water frontage but is usually located near or within walking distance of the waterfront.

- **Bottomlands:** The ground or earth located under a body of water.

- **Broker's Fee:** The percentage of the sales price paid (usually at closing) to a realtor, real estate agent, or other broker or agent. Whether some or all of these fees are paid by the buyer, seller, or both (as well as the amount of such fees) can be a source of negotiation. Such fees should be specified in the purchase/sales agreement.

- **Buildability:** The ability of a property to have a dwelling built thereon, an existing dwelling replaced, or to add onto an existing building. This can refer to physical limitations on the property as well as zoning or other ordinance or legal restrictions.

- **Chain of Title:** All prior deeds, easements, land contracts, deed restrictions, restrictive covenants, etc. (which have normally been recorded with the county register of deeds) regarding the property at issue.

- **Closing:** The climax or final step of a real estate transaction. Typically, the buyer of the waterfront property transfers the purchase funds to the seller and the seller gives a deed or land contract to the buyer at closing.

- **Closing Costs:** Items that must be paid at closing (apart from the purchase price) and which can include, but are not limited to, real estate transfer taxes, recording fees, document preparation fees, title insurance costs, mortgage fees, and survey fee.

- **Closing Statement:** A written breakdown of the costs involved in a real estate transaction for signing at closing. Typically, there is both a seller's closing statement and a buyer's closing statement at closing.

- **Cloud on Title:** Something recorded with the county register of deeds regarding the property at issue that involves a liability or makes the property less valuable or attractive. This can include liens, false claims, and similar matters.

- **Condominium:** This is a type of ownership that is different than that to which most people are accustomed. In a condominium project, individual landowners own a "unit." The developer, and later the condominium association, owns the common areas such as the roads, recreation facilities, etc. Conventional condominiums include duplexes, fourplexes, and multiple-family buildings where individual property owners own one "unit" or an air space within the complex. Areas such as common stairs, walkways, elevators, etc., are owned in common. In the past few decades, a new form of development, the "site condominium," has arisen in Michigan. Site condominiums resemble traditional plats or housing developments, but have a strong property owners association and certain properties are owned in common.

- **Contingency:** A clause or provision inserted into a purchase/sales agreement that allows one or both of the parties to cancel the agreement (and not proceed to closing) if certain conditions do not occur, events do not transpire, or requirements cannot be met before closing.

- **Covenant:** A formal agreement or contract that relates to real estate.

- **Deed:** A written document given by the seller to the property purchaser to transfer title to a piece of property. Once the purchaser of a property has the deed, it is normally recorded with the county register of deeds. A deed can be a warranty deed (where good title is warranted by the seller) or a quitclaim deed (no title warranties).

- **Deeded Access:** This is a somewhat misleading term. It usually means that a backlot property has some type of legally-existing lake or river access located nearby that is shared with a few or many other people. However, such accesses are rarely contained within the deed or chain of title to the backlot.

- **Deed Restrictions:** Also sometimes known as covenants or restrictive covenants. These are rules and regulations that have been recorded with the county register of deeds and limit uses, activities, and other matters that can occur on a property or series of properties. Usually, they are permanent and "run with the land."

- **Dock:** A structure or item typically made of wood, metal, or plastic-type decking material that extends into a lake or river, and assists with boat or watercraft mooring, anchoring, or navigability. If you were born and live north of an east-west line that intersects Kalamazoo, such structures are typically referred to as a "dock." If you live south of that line (or you are a visitor from Ohio, Indiana, or Illinois), the word "dock" is not in your vocabulary, and instead, you use the non-Michigan word "pier."

- **Earnest Money:** Typically, a minimal down payment paid by the prospective purchaser of a property to the seller (or third-party escrow agent) at the time the purchase/sales agreement is signed, which is applied to the purchase price at closing or, if the transaction does not close, it may or may not be refundable to the prospective purchaser.

- **Easement:** The right of someone to permanently use the property of another for a specific limited purpose. Easements can be utilized for utilities, waterfront access, driveways, private roads, and other uses.

- **Encroachment:** When something attributable to one property is physically located on the adjoining property. Encroachments can include buildings, structures, septic systems, easements, driveways, sidewalks, landscaping, and similar items.

- **Encumbrances:** These are legal items that attach to real estate or the title to real estate. They are almost always negative aspects to the owner of the property. Encumbrances can include liens, easements, deed restrictions or restrictive covenants, construction liens, mortgages, rights of first refusal, and special assessments.

- **Equity:** The word "equity" in real estate can have at least two different meanings. First, equity is often used to mean the unencumbered value one has in a piece of real estate. That is, a property owner's "equity" in real estate is the difference between what the real estate is worth on the open market (what it can be sold for during an ordinary arms-length transaction) and the monetary sum of all mortgages, liens, and other monetary encumbrances on the property. In other words, if you sell your property, it is the net amount of money you can put in your pocket after the sale closes. Second, equity also means the power of a court in litigation involving real estate to order someone to do or not do something (for example, ordering a purchase/sales agreement to proceed based on specific performance, the issuance of an injunction prohibiting a house from being torn down, etc.).

- **Erosion:** The washing away of land, shoreline, banks, or similar earth by rain or water action.

- **Escrow:** This occurs when a neutral third party (for example, a title insurance company) holds certain monies of one or both parties to a real estate transaction in a fund, with such monies eventually being disbursed pursuant to the strict requirements of a signed escrow agreement. One example involves earnest money. Earnest money paid by the purchaser pursuant to the signing of a purchase/sales agreement is often deposited with a title insurance company acting as a third-party escrow agent. If the transaction closes, the escrow agent releases the earnest money, which is applied to the purchase price. If the closing does not occur due to no fault of the purchaser, the earnest money is returned to the purchaser. If the purchaser breaches the purchase/sales agreement, the earnest money is often paid to the seller as all or part of the seller's remedy.

- **Estate:** Technically, in Michigan, a person does not own real estate, but rather, an estate in land. An estate is the type, nature, degree, amount, or quality of a person's interest in real estate. There are many different types of estates in Michigan, including a fee simple absolute estate, a life estate, a conditional estate, and others.

- **Fee Simple Absolute Title:** This is the best title to real estate that a person can obtain in Michigan. Generally, this means an unencumbered, fully-marketable title.

- **Fixture:** Technically, this is not real estate, but personal property. A fixture is an item attached to land or a building that is normally considered an unmovable part of the real estate. Outdoor fixtures can include fences, towers, light poles, and similar items.

- **Homestead Exemption:** Under Proposal A in Michigan, real property taxes are lower for a person's residence as a result of the "Homestead Exemption" which provides an 18-mill reduction in the property tax rate. This typically equates to 30%-40% of the total tax bill depending on the base tax rate of the local municipality. The Homestead Exemption is now referred to as the "Principal Residence Exemption" or "PRE."

- **Land Contract:** A land contract is used in place of a deed. A land contract involves a financing method whereby the seller of real property finances the purchaser's acquisition of the real property. Only after the land contract has been paid off does the seller give a deed to the purchaser.

- **Lead-Based Paint Disclosure Act:** The federal Residential Lead-Based Paint Hazard Reduction Act of 1992 requires sellers to disclose in writing the presence of lead-based paint to the prospective purchaser of the dwelling under certain circumstances.

- **Lien:** A type of real estate encumbrance. A right or interest that a lender or creditor has in another person's property, which usually secures a debt or obligation. Normally, the lienholder (the lien's beneficiary) does not take possession of the land until and unless the lien is "foreclosed" or pursued via court action or other legal procedure.

- **Lis Pendens:** A document recorded with the county register of deeds indicating that the property is currently the subject of litigation (usually called a "notice lis pendens").

- **Listing:** This is shorthand for a realtor or real estate agent representing the seller of a particular property. It means that a property for sale is "listed with" a particular realtor or real estate agent.

- **Listing Agreement:** This is an agreement entered into between a broker (typically, a real estate agent or realtor) and a buyer or seller of real estate. It is a broker agreement, which specifies the terms of the broker-agent relationship.

- **Littoral:** A property with frontage on a lake. This term is rarely used today. It has been replaced with the broader word, "riparian."

- **Marketable Title:** Lay people refer to this as "good and proper" title to real property. In the legal sense, marketable title is defined as legal title to a piece of real estate that is reasonable because it lacks any significant defect and would allow the purchaser to later freely sell the real estate (and title to it) without encumbrances or obstacles. Sometimes also referred to as "clear title."

- **Metes and Bounds:** Technical language used by a surveyor to describe the location and boundary lines of a parcel that is not a platted lot or condominium unit. Metes and bounds legal descriptions can be found in a deed, land contract, or survey. A typical metes and bounds legal description might start out "Commencing at the southwest corner of Section 2 of Township 5 North, Range 6 West, Acme Township, Kent County, Michigan, thence North 21°23'05" West 237 feet, thence south 01°53'23" East 93.7 feet …."

- **Memorandum of Land Contract:** Given the extensive information contained in a land contract (some of it potentially sensitive), parties to a land contract often do not want to record the land contract itself with the local county register of deeds where everyone can read it after recording. Instead, the parties can sign a document entitled a "memorandum of land contract" (which contains a legal description for the property involved, the seller's name, the buyer's name, and limited other information), which is recorded for public notice with the county register of deeds in lieu of recording the land contract itself.

- **Mineral Rights:** This is one of many real property rights and it can be severed from the ownership of the surface of the land. Mineral rights typically include the rights to mine or extract oil, gas, gravel, sand, and other valuable minerals.

- **Mortgage:** A written instrument that is recorded with the county register of deeds regarding a particular property evidencing that the owner of the property (typically, the purchaser) has borrowed money from a bank or other financial institution. The mortgage is the public evidence of that loan and "secures" the loan. It is one type of lien.

- **Mortgage Survey:** Not a true survey, or at least not a survey that is up to the normal standards. These are typically ordered by lending institutions prior to money being loaned pursuant to a mortgage.

- **Multiple Listing Service:** Often called the "MLS." Typically, this is a trade or marketing organization comprised of a group of realtors or real estate agents who pool their respective listings. The MLS allows a realtor or real estate broker to have access to a wide variety of listings of other realtors or brokers. There are many regional MLS systems within the country. In most cases, in order for a broker to have a listing on the MLS, the broker must be properly licensed and belong to an organization such as the National Association of Realtors. Landowners who attempt to sell their property without a broker or real estate agent usually cannot list their property on an MLS.

- **Navigability:** In common usage, the ability to utilize a boat on a body of water. Incidents of navigability include boating and fishing.

- **Ordinary High Water Mark (also known as the Normal High Water Mark):** Theoretically, each lake has a point on the shore that constitutes the average water mark or water level over a number of years. On some lakes and certain waterfront properties, experts disagree as to what constitutes the specific ordinary high water mark.

- **Perc Test:** This is short for a "percolation test." In the past, it was utilized by the local health department to determine whether or not a property was suitable for an on-site private septic system. A perc test involved digging a hole, pouring water into the hole, and measuring how long it would take for the water to "percolate" down into the soil. Today, most public health departments utilize other tests to determine the suitability of a property for a private on-site septic system.

- **Personal Property Tax:** This is not a tax on real estate, but on commercial items, products, etc. It only applies to businesses in Michigan, not residential or nonbusiness properties.

- **Pier:** See also "dock." In Michigan vernacular, piers tend to be larger than docks, are usually permanent (with pilings), and are frequently found in the Great Lakes or large inland lakes that are tied into the Great Lakes. If you are from south of Kalamazoo (particularly, from Ohio, Indiana, or Illinois), you probably use the word "pier" to mean "dock." Most people in Michigan prefer the word "dock" for seasonal small structures.

- **Plat:** One form of development or subdivision. Typically, a lot in a plat will be described as "Lot 1 of the Acme Plat ...."

- **Points:** Banks, mortgage companies, and lending institutions frequently allow a purchaser of real estate who is financing the purchase by a mortgage to be subject to a lower interest rate over the life of the loan by "buying down" the loan or "paying points" at closing. As used in this context, one "point" represents 1% of the loan amount (one-half of a point equals .5% of the loan amount, one-quarter point equals .25% of the loan amount, etc.). For example, suppose that the purchaser is borrowing $100,000 to finance a real estate purchase, and that the normal interest rate for the 30-year loan desired is 6%, but with payment of a point, the rate is 5.75%. That is, the particular bank involved will lower the interest rate by one-quarter of 1% in exchange for the borrower paying one point. Therefore, by paying an additional $1,000 (or one point) at the closing, the land purchaser would be lowering the long-term interest rate for the loan from 6% down to 5.75%. Lending institutions vary in how generous they will be in lowering the interest rate (by what rate reduction) when the borrower pays one point. Depending on the transaction involved, points may or may not be allowed to be deducted on the real estate purchaser's income taxes.

- **"Pop-Up" (or "Uncapping"):** No, this is not a toaster pastry! Under Michigan's real property taxation laws (adopted by Michigan voters pursuant to Proposal A), tax assessments on real property can only go up annually by the rate of inflation or 5%, whichever is less. Accordingly, after a few years, with appreciating real property values, the "capped" property tax assessment for a given property is generally much lower than the market value (actually, to compare, both numbers must be cut in half, as property is assessed only at 50% of its value). However, the property tax assessment is allowed to "float" once there is a sale or transfer of title for the property. That results in a "pop-up" or "uncapping" of the assessed valuation of the real estate for property tax purposes.

- **Proration of Property Taxes:** This involves determining what portion of the property taxes a seller will pay at closing versus the percentage to be paid by the buyer at closing. If the purchase/sales agreement simply provides that the seller will pay all real property tax bills sent out before closing and that the buyer will pay all property tax bills sent out after the closing, no proration occurs. Proration is the utilization of a formula for determining which party pays how much of the property taxes at closing. In most instances in Michigan, property taxes are prorated on a "calendar year basis."

- **Quitclaim Deed:** This is a type of deed for which no warranty or guarantee of title is given by the seller. The seller is simply indicating that any title the seller has to a particular piece of property (if any), the seller is transferring to the buyer. Title insurance is particularly important for transactions involving quitclaim deeds.

- **Real Estate Agent:** An agent or broker who represents a buyer or seller of land (or both, with proposer disclosure) with regard to the sale or lease of real estate. Technically, a real estate agent is not the same as a real estate broker, despite the interchange of those phrases by lay people. More specifically, a real estate agent can be either a broker (whose principal is generally a buyer or seller of real estate) or a salesperson (whose principal is normally a broker).

- **Real Estate Broker:** Someone who is hired by a person to serve as an agent or broker in connection with real estate transactions (which can include the sale, lease, renting, purchase, or trading of real property). The person hiring the broker or agent is sometimes referred to as the "principal."

- **Real Estate Property Transfer Tax:** Pursuant to Michigan statute, there are two real estate transfer taxes. These taxes are paid pursuant to the transfer of title to real property by deed, land contract, or memorandum of land contract. The state real property transfer tax is levied at $3.75 per $500 of consideration paid. The county transfer tax is levied at $.55 per $500 of consideration paid. (Assumed mortgages of the seller constitute "consideration paid" for purpose of calculating transfer tax.)

- **Real Property:** This is a technical term for land. "Personal property" involves nonland items such as cars, furniture, boats, bank accounts, etc. A "fixture" is a property interest in between real property and personal property. A fixture is an item attached to real property such as a fence, sign, or similar item.

- **Realtor:** A special type of real estate agent or broker. Normally, a member of the National Association of Realtors.

- **Recording:** The act of taking and filing a real estate document with the county register of deeds. This gives "public notice" to everyone of the recorded document. Every document must be in a particular format for recording. The county register of deeds charges a fee to the person who wishes to have a document recorded. Once the document has been accepted by the county register of deeds for recording, the office "stamps" certain information on the document and inputs a copy of the document into the computer. Once a document is recorded, any member of the public can view a copy of the document. After a few weeks or months, the original of the document (with the county register of deeds "stamp" on it) is returned to the person designated on the document (usually the land purchaser).

- **Register of Deeds:** A governmental office or agency found in every county government in Michigan. Real estate documents are "recorded" with the local register of deeds office for the county in which the property is located. These recorded document copies are open to the public.

- **Reliction:** The receding of water from a shoreline or bank. It is a process whereby bottomlands are exposed.

- **Right of First Refusal:** This is a type of option that indicates that before a property can be sold or transferred to a third party, it must first be offered to the person or persons designated with a right of first refusal. Only if such person or persons refuse to purchase the property can the property be transferred or sold to a third party. This is often also referred to as a first option or first refusal right.

- **Riparian:** Technically, a property with frontage on a flowing body of water such as a river, creek, or stream. In common everyday usage, riparian has come to mean a waterfront property on a lake, river, stream, or creek. Also sometimes used to refer to the owner of a waterfront property.

- **Riparian Boundary Line:** Where the bottomland ownership of one riparian or waterfront property owner leaves off and the ownership of another begins.

- **Road Ends:** These are public road rights-of-way or private road easements that are perpendicular to or end at a body of water. The lake usage rights for such road ends are often very limited.

- **Runs With the Land:** This phrase means that a particular item (for example, an easement, deed restriction/restrictive covenant, or other obligation) permanently binds the land involved, and binds not only the current owner of the property, but also all future owners of the property as well.

- **Seller's Disclosure Statement:** A filled-out form that a seller of a property with a dwelling thereon must provide to the buyer before closing as required by Michigan statute (MCL 565.951).

- **Septic System:** This is shorthand for an on-site private septic system. This type of system must be utilized where a public sanitary sewer hookup is not available. The phrase "septic system" is normally shorthand for the entire system, which can include a septic tank, drain field, piping, sand, gravel, etc.

- **Setbacks:** This refers to how far a building, structure, well, or septic system must be located from another item, such as the ordinary high water mark of a body of water, lot lines, the road, or other reference points. Such regulations can be contained in deed restrictions, zoning or other ordinances, and health department regulations.

- **Site Condominium:** This is a relatively new form of condominium project. It resembles a plat or conventional residential development. Rather than owning a lot or parcel, a landowner owns a "unit." As with any condominium, a site condominium contains commonly-owned and used properties such as a private road, recreational facilities, and sidewalks.

- **Special Assessment (Special Assessment District):** These are like taxes. They are set up by the local government for a particular area, neighborhood, or region to fund public improvements or services such as aquatic weed treatment in lakes, the installation of sidewalks, fire department services, the improvement of roads, street lighting, and other projects. Not all properties have special assessments. Special assessments usually appear on the real property tax bills. Normally, the special assessment component of a property tax bill is not deductible on the property owner's state or federal income taxes.

- **Specific Performance:** This is a court remedy (equitable in nature) available to either a purchaser or seller of property where the other party violates a purchase/sales agreement. In most cases, it orders the closing to proceed. Specific performance is usually implemented by a court via a mandatory injunction or court order ordering someone to do or not do something.

- **Statute of Frauds:** In Michigan, no agreement or contract regarding the sale, purchase, or transfer of real estate (or any interest therein) is valid unless it is in a writing signed by all parties. The statute also applies to leases over one year. See MCL 566.106, 556.108, and 556.132.

- **Survey:** Work performed by a professional surveyor or engineer who examines the property involved, maps out various features of the property (such as size, location of boundary lines and easements, and similar matters), creates or verifies the legal description for the property, places irons and stakes on the land, and draws a survey map.

- **Taxable Value:** This is a real property tax phrase. The actual property tax paid on a given property annually is based on the taxable value multiplied by a certain percentage (which represents the millage rate). Under Proposal A, the annual assessment (as represented by taxable value) cannot annually increase by more than 5% or the rate of inflation, whichever is less. By law, the taxable value "uncaps" following a sale or transfer of ownership of the property.

- **Tax Proration:** See "Proration of Property Taxes."

- **Title Insurance Commitment:** This is a written commitment or promise by a title insurance company that it will issue a particular title insurance policy if a real estate closing occurs. Title insurance commitments are typically ordered and provided after the purchase/sales agreement has been signed but well in advance of closing. A title insurance commitment will show what kind of title the seller has to a particular piece of property, as well as list any mortgages, encumbrances, liens, deed restrictions, easements, etc.

- **Title Insurance:** Title insurance is provided to a purchaser of real property to ensure a particular title to that property. In most cases, the seller pays for the title insurance, which is provided to the purchaser after closing. Title insurance only covers the matters listed in the title insurance policy and certain matters can be excluded via that policy. Should a defect in title or similar matter arise later (which was insured against via the title insurance policy), the title insurance company will attempt to remedy the problem, either via negotiation or by court action.

- **To the Water's Edge:** This phrase is often used in legal descriptions for waterfront property. In most cases, if this or similar language is used in Michigan, it means it is a lakefront property and that the property also contains or has certain bottomlands under the water to the center of the lake, river, or stream.

- **Warranty Deed:** A deed that gives certain warranties or guaranties of title and other matters. The warranty is only as good as the seller or the title insurance (if any) covering the warranty.

- **Waste:** Permanent or significant harm done to the property of another by the lawful possessor of the property. Waste is usually committed by a tenant or land contract buyer.

- **Water View or Lake View Property:** Not a property with frontage on a lake or river, but a property where a person can see the waterfront from the property. This type of property can often be located some distance from the waterfront and may only mean that the owner has a sliver of a view of the water from far away.

- **Zoning Ordinance or Zoning Regulations:** This is a specific type of local government regulation authorized by the Michigan Zoning Enabling Act, being MCL 125.3101 *et seq.* Other types of ordinances enacted by local governments include "police power" ordinances, which are not zoning regulations. In general, zoning regulations tend to regulate uses of land, structures, and buildings, whereas police power ordinances usually regulate activities.

Chapter 43
ESTATE PLANNING AND KEEPING THE FAMILY WATERFRONT PROPERTY IN THE FAMILY

ONCE YOU PURCHASE A WATERFRONT PROPERTY, YOU should carefully contemplate what will happen to it if you should still own it upon your death. Waterfront properties in Michigan are not like other properties or lands. More often than not, they evoke sentimentality and quite often, a desire to keep the property in the family indefinitely. For those riparians who wish to eventually pass their lakefront property on to their children, nieces, nephews, grandchildren, or others, estate planning is particularly important. Estate planning tools for that purpose can include wills, trusts, limited liability companies, and other documents, techniques, and entities.

Of course, estate planning basics include having an up-to-date will and where a waterfront property is involved, at the very least, a well-drafted trust. Without having at least these documents (or other estate planning documents) in place when a riparian property owner dies, it often guarantees that a beloved waterfront property will not stay in the family, or if it does, will cause infighting among the heirs and potentially others. In addition, the time-honored (or rather, dishonored) technique of simply placing children, grandchildren, or others on the title to the waterfront property via a deed or deeds as a way of doing "cheap" estate planning often leads to disaster (which can include such horror scenarios as severe tax consequences, the inability to reverse the situation while the parent is still alive if one of the children refuses to sign off, a share in the property going to a spouse who has divorced the riparian property owner's child, etc.).

For Michigan estate planning techniques and background with regard to waterfront property, the late attorney Stuart Hollander's publication entitled *Saving the Family Cottage – A Guide to Succession Planning for your Cottage, Cabin, Camp or Vacation Home* is particularly helpful. That guide can alert riparian property owners to some of the basics before they meet with their own estate planning attorneys.

If title to a waterfront property will eventually go to more than one person via estate planning when the current riparian property owner or owners die, then either a trust or a limited liability company should normally be utilized. A will alone is not usually sufficient or well-equipped to deal with the countless issues that will likely arise in the future. Those issues can include, but are not necessarily limited to, the following:

- Allocation of property costs among owners such as utility bills, property taxes, upkeep and repair, improvements, etc.
- Voting procedures among owners.
- What happens to a person's share upon divorce, bankruptcy, disability, death, etc.?
- What happens if one of the future owners goes bankrupt or is being pursued by creditors?
- "Buyout" provisions if a future co-owner wants "out."
- Ability of the property to be mortgaged.
- A prohibition on "partition" (a judicial proceeding to divide the property or order the property sold and the proceeds distributed).
- A possible "end date" for the arrangement (what happens if 50 years from now, the property is co-owned by 47 different heirs and they cannot agree on anything?).
- Limits on the ability of co-owners to sell or transfer their interest to people outside of the family.
- How to handle major improvements to the property (such as replacing the cabin or cottage, adding on to the dwelling, the need for a new septic system or well, etc.).

At the current time, limited liability companies are generally favored over trusts for waterfront property estate planning purposes. However, that could change as Michigan statutes are amended, tax laws are altered, etc.

Estate planning with regard to waterfront property is one area where the property owner should not attempt to "go it on their own" — a skilled estate planning attorney who is well-versed in waterfront properties, wills, trusts, limited liability companies, and similar techniques is essential. Paying a professional to do it right now will likely save many times that amount later, as well as potentially keep families from destroying themselves over the waterfront property in the future.

Chapter 44
CONDOMINIUMS

FREQUENTLY, LAKEFRONT PROPERTIES IN MICHIGAN
are located in condominium developments. A condominium
can be defined as a form of property ownership or development
where a landowner holds title to an individual unit together with
a fractional share or interest in common areas or elements (such
as roads, playgrounds, recreation facilities, and similar items). A
strong property owners association governs the common areas
and other matters. Condominiums can be high-rise apartment-like
buildings, duplexes, or single unit properties that resemble lots
in a subdivision. In Michigan, condominium developments are
governed by the Michigan Condominium Act, being MCL 559.101
et seq.

A prospective purchaser of a unit in a condominium must be
particularly vigilant. State regulation is minimal. Condominiums
are subject to a comprehensive set of deed restrictions/restrictive
covenants contained in the condominium documents (which
are usually comprised of a master deed, site plan or plans,
condominium bylaws, association bylaws, and other documents).
Condominium documents are frequently voluminous. Prior to
closing, the condominium documents should be extensively and
carefully reviewed by the prospective purchaser or that purchaser's
attorney, and there should be a contingency clause contained

within the purchase/sales agreement that allows the purchaser to cancel the real estate purchase if the buyer is not fully satisfied with the condominium documents before closing.

Several decades ago, a new type of condominium emerged in Michigan called a "site condominium." Site condominiums resemble conventional single-family subdivisions. The site condominium concept was validated by the Michigan Attorney General in a formal opinion dated March 13, 1989 (OAG No. 6577).

Due to the extensive deed restrictions, rules, and regulations governing condominiums, what an individual unit owner can do is often severely limited. Such restrictions can often protect property values and enhance the waterfront living experience. However, if the idea of living in a tightly-controlled community with a strong property owners association and extensive deed restrictions does not appeal to you, don't buy a condominium unit!

Chapter 45
LAKE ASSOCIATIONS

There is no universally-acknowledged or accepted definition of a lake association in Michigan. A rough definition could include a group of landowners at, on, or near a lake who have organized to promote their best interests and the welfare of the lake.

There are generally two kinds of lake associations in Michigan — some that I call "strong" lake associations, and others which I have labeled "weak" associations. Strong lake associations typically fall into one of two categories. First, there are some lakes (particularly artificially-created lakes) whereby all of the lakefront properties are bound or governed by a comprehensive set of recorded deed restrictions or restrictive covenants. In some cases, those deed restrictions create a mandatory lake association and give it extensive powers. The second type of strong lake association involves an association created pursuant to one of Michigan's ancient summer resort statutes. Those statutes vest a properly-constituted summer resort association with quasi-municipal powers. Duly-constituted summer resort associations are actually relatively rare. Strong lake associations probably account for less than 5% of the total number of lake associations in Michigan.

Most lake associations in Michigan are "weak" associations. That is, riparian property owners join on a voluntary basis and the only "powers" held by such associations are those voluntarily consented to by the members.

Structurally, lake associations are of general two types — incorporated and unincorporated. Incorporated lake associations are usually nonprofit corporations set up pursuant to the Michigan Nonprofit Corporation Act, being MCLA 450.2101 *et seq.* A corporate entity actually exists which, theoretically, has a life span and existence in addition to and apart from its membership. If a lake association has not been incorporated, it is simply a voluntary nonentity existing in name only.

Depending upon how they are set up, strong associations often have dues-making and enforcement powers, while weak associations can only collect dues on a voluntary basis. I am frequently asked whether there is any way to make dues paying mandatory in a weak association. The answer is normally "no," unless the voluntary association is able to prompt the creation of a summer resort association or convince all riparian property owners on the lake involved to sign a comprehensive set of new deed restrictions. Either scenario is unlikely with most lakes. If the bulk of the association's dues goes for aquatic weed treatment purposes, a weak association can sometimes convince the local municipality to set up a special assessment district for weed treatment purposes. If a special assessment district is created, the municipality collects mandatory assessments via the property tax bill which are akin to dues for aquatic weed treatment purposes (except that the money is collected and spent by the local municipality rather than the lake association).

Although incorporation of a weak association is not mandatory, it is advisable. Incorporation formalizes the existence of a lake association and helps insulate officers and members of the association against potential personal liability (although such a liability shield is not absolute). Incorporation also has other potential benefits, including the ability of the association to obtain liability insurance and utilize bank accounts, making it easier to institute court action should the need arise, and creating "standing" in administrative agency proceedings (like proceedings before the Michigan Department of Natural Resources and the Environment).

Lake associations in Michigan run the gamut from small, loosely-knit groups of people to formal, well-organized incorporated organizations. The following is a list of general organizational types of lake associations, although there can be "overlap" between different categories:

- Unincorporated associations or informal groups of property owners.

- An association which is incorporated as a Michigan nonprofit corporation.

- A condominium association.

- An association or compilation of two or more neighborhood, lake, area, or similar organizations or associations.

- A summer resort and assembly association, a suburban homestead, villa park, and summer resort association, or a summer resort association (based on several old Michigan statutes).

- A limited liability corporation.

For more information about Michigan lake associations, please see my other Michigan Lake & Stream Associations, Inc. ("ML&SA") publication, *Michigan Lake Associations — The Nuts and Bolts*, available at www.mymlsa.org or by contacting ML&SA or by using the form at Attachment L.

Chapter 46
WHY YOU AND YOUR LAKE ASSOCIATION SHOULD JOIN THE MICHIGAN LAKE & STREAM ASSOCIATIONS, INC.

THE MICHIGAN LAKE & STREAM ASSOCIATIONS, Inc. ("ML&SA") is the largest group in the state of Michigan representing lake associations, river associations, and individuals with waterfront property. Joining ML&SA accords individuals and lake associations many benefits and privileges, including the following:

- The ability to attend a valuable annual statewide convention and helpful regional seminars.

- Access to a variety of educational and resource materials regarding lakes, lake watersheds, legal issues involving lakes, etc.

- Assistance with your lake association website.

- Access to the very informative ML&SA website.

- The ability of your association to have scientific and technical questions answered by limnologists, aquatic biologists and other professionals.

- ML&SA works on behalf of associations and riparian land owners as an advocate for the preservation and management of our inland lakes, streams and water resources, as well as the protection of your riparian property rights.

ML&SA has an excellent website that can be accessed at www.mymlsa.org. Membership applications are available for download from the website.

Chapter 47
THE MICHIGAN RIPARIAN MAGAZINE

The Michigan Riparian is the foremost publication that deals with lake, river, stream, and water resources in Michigan. It is published four times annually. Back issues and articles can also be viewed at *The Michigan Riparian* website at www.mi-riparian.org.

The Michigan Riparian is in its 47th year of publication. Special lake association and group rates are available. If you have an idea for a future article for the magazine or would like to submit a "letter to the editor," please send an email to info@mi-riparian.org or mail your idea or letter to *The Michigan Riparian* at 304 East Main Street, Stanton, Michigan 48888. See Attachment M for a subscription form.

Chapter 48
THE MICHIGAN WATERFRONT ALLIANCE

The Michigan Waterfront Alliance ("MWA") is an advocacy and lobbying entity that although related to ML&SA, is a separate and distinct organization and has the ability to influence legislation through lobbying (an activity which ML&SA, a 501(c)(3) organization, generally cannot pursue). MWA's mission is to preserve and protect riparian rights for waterfront landowners throughout Michigan. It is the only statewide unified advocacy voice to protect Michigan's lakes and streams. Some of the issues which MWA has dealt with include invasive species, water rights, DNRE lake access/property acquisitions, marine safety, environmental protection, unreasonable resource use, and lobbying for riparian rights.

MWA has been instrumental in preventing adverse road end legislation from being enacted by the Michigan Legislature that would have fostered lake overuse by enabling road end marinas at virtually every public road end in the state of Michigan. MWA has also filed several amicus curiae briefs with the Michigan appellate courts (including the Michigan Supreme Court) to protect and defend riparian rights throughout Michigan.

For a number of years, MWA has retained a lobbying firm to advocate for the best interests of Michigan's riparian property owners and to protect the state's lakes and streams.

Members of MWA receive various benefits including the assistance of a professional lobbyist in Lansing to protect riparian interests, periodic mailed newsletters, advocacy at important legislative hearings and meetings, lobbyist reports, email action alerts, and much more.

Visit MWA's website at www.mwai.org. To join MWA, please make a copy of the application at Attachment N, fill it out, and send the completed application together with the membership fee to the address listed on the form.

Chapter 49
ADDITIONAL
RESOURCES

The Michigan Lake & Stream Associations, Inc.'s publication *Michigan Lake Associations – The Nuts and Bolts*, authored by Cliff Bloom, is a valuable resources for any waterfront property owner. Please see Attachment L for more information about that book.

For more information about lake associations, lakes, and aquatic matters in general in Michigan, you should consider subscribing to *The Michigan Riparian* magazine. A subscription form for the magazine is attached as Attachment M. Furthermore, you can visit *The Michigan Riparian* website at www.mi-riparian.org.

Following is a list of the articles I have authored for *The Michigan Riparian* magazine from the early 1990s through the summer 2011 issue of the magazine. Those articles (together with articles from more recent issues of the magazine) can be read or obtained at *The Michigan Riparian* website.

- No Good Deed Goes Unpunished!
- Dock Permits: Michigan Lakes Tied into the Great Lakes
- Two More Interesting Lake Access Easement Cases
- 2001 *Baum Family Trust v Babel* — R.I.P.

- The Beach Walker Case
- No More Excuses for Municipalities
- Why is Insurance Important
- But my Realtor Told Me ...
- Recent Michigan Appellate Cases of Interest
- Liability Concerns
- Recent Events
- Blueprint to Protect your Lake
- Current Topics of Interest
- Pro-Riparian Michigan Appellate Court Cases Regarding Lake Access Easements
- Wither Ice Mountain?
- Lake Front Legal Issues
- The Top Eleven Threats
- An Overview of Riparian Issues
- Michigan Supreme Court Decision
- On Water — Does Anything Go?
- Amicus Curiae Briefs
- Recent Cases of Interest
- Adverse Possession and Prescriptive Easements
- Riparian Rights and Other Legal Matters
- Zoning Tools

- What Hath the Michigan Court of Appeals Wrought?
- Maximum Enforcement
- Funneling — Bad!
- The Top Ten Excuses — Are you Kidding?
- Getting in the Zone
- Properties Boundaries
- Who Pulled the Plug?
- Keeping it in the Family
- Trespass!
- What Happens if the Dog Catches the Car?
- Survey Stakes on the Lake Front?!!!
- Dormant Lake Access Devices — Let Sleeping Dogs Lie?
- Lake Access/Keyhole Ordinances
- One Definition of Chutzpah
- Dock Wars
- A Modest Proposal
- What is Navigability?
- Urban Sprawl
- What Can be Done About Jet Skis?
- Recent Enacted Statutes and Current Issues
- What to do About Unreasonably Long Docks
- Preemption and Local Control

- Public Accesses — Rights and Limitations
- Permit Requirements
- Trojan Horse
- Drainage Issues
- Weed Control
- Incorporation
- Road Ends
- No Lake Access

The ML&SA website can be found at www.mymlsa.org. The Michigan Waterfront Alliance's website is www.mwai.org. Also feel free to stop by at ML&SA's state office in Stanton at 306 E. Main Street, Stanton, Michigan 48888, or call ML&SA at (989) 831-5100.

* * *

Attachment O is a helpful checklist of lake property characteristics that can help a prospective purchaser determine what type of a property he or she really wants.

Attachments

Attachment A
DUE DILIGENCE CHECKLIST AND POTENTIAL ISSUES

1. **Before the purchase/sales agreement is signed:**

   _____ Do you really want waterfront property?

   _____ What type of waterfront land do you want to purchase (inland lake, Great Lakes, river, creek/stream, or other)?

   _____ Choosing the proper realtor/real estate agent.

   _____ Finding a capable real estate attorney (optional).

   _____ What can you afford?

   _____ "Prequalifying" for financing.

   _____ In what geographical area do you want the property to be?

   _____ Arrangements to sell your existing house (optional).

   _____ Negotiating a purchase/sales agreement (and all applicable contingencies).

   _____ Potential tax consequences.

2. **During the time period between the signing of the purchase/sales agreement and closing.**

   _____ Dwelling inspection.

   _____ Property inspections.

   _____ Reviewing the title insurance commitment.

_____ Firming up the financing.

_____ Consulting with experts (attorney, engineer, home inspector, etc.).

_____ Having a survey done.

_____ Local government reviews for a new dwelling or expansion (zoning, septic, well, etc.).

_____ Vacant parcel-buildability issues must be addressed.

_____ Satisfying other contingencies.

Attachment B
BUYER'S CHECKLIST—
GENERAL APPROACH

1. Decide what types and locations of waterfront property to purchase.

2. Preliminary arrangement for financing (where applicable).

3. How much can I afford?

4. Select a realtor/real estate agent.

5. Negotiate a purchase/sales agreement.

    (a) Earnest money.

    (b) Contingencies.

    (c) Miscellaneous clauses.

6. Sign the negotiated purchase/sales agreement.

7. [Optional: Amendment or addendum to the purchase/sales agreement.]

8. Receive and review seller's disclosure statement (if there is a dwelling).

9. Receive and review the title insurance commitment.

10. Have all inspections and reports done.

    (a) Existing dwelling.

    (b) Vacant land evaluations.

11. Perform all due diligence before closing.

12. Satisfaction/nonsatisfaction of contingencies in the purchase/sales agreement.

13. Change utilities.

14. Closing:

    (a) Purchase money.

    (b) Sign all documents.

    (c) Deed or land contract.

15. Post-closing matters.

    (a) Possession.

    (b) Homeowners insurance.

    (c) Keep closing documents in a safe place forever!

    (d) Receive final title insurance.

Attachment C
PURCHASE/SALES AGREEMENT FORM (SAMPLE)

REAL ESTATE PURCHASE/SALES AGREEMENT

THIS REAL ESTATE PURCHASE/SALES AGREEMENT (this "Agreement") is entered into on this _____ day of_____, 20___, between __ _____, of _____ _____ ("Seller") and _____ _____, of _____ _____ ("Buyer") upon the following terms and conditions:

1. Description of Property. Seller agrees to sell to Buyer and Buyer agrees to purchase from Seller the improved real property located in _____ Michigan, commonly known as _____ _____, PPN _____, [**Optional**—and legally described on Exhibit A as attached hereto] together with all improvements, buildings and fixtures, and subject to easements and restrictions of record, if any (the "Property").

2. Purchase Price. The purchase price for the Property is $_____, subject to any debits or credits as set forth herein, and payable in immediately available funds at closing (the "Purchase Price").

3. Earnest Money. [As of the date this Agreement is signed, Seller acknowledges receipt of the sum of $_____ from Buyer to be held by Seller as a good faith earnest money deposit (the "Deposit")] OR [Within five days of full execution of this Agreement, Buyer must deposit $_____ in escrow with the title company issuing the title insurance policy referenced below as a good faith earnest money deposit (the "Deposit").] The Deposit is applicable to the Purchase Price upon closing if the transaction covered by this Agreement proceeds to closing.

4. Payment of Purchase Price. Buyer shall pay the full Purchase Price to Seller at the closing upon execution and delivery of a [Warranty/ Quitclaim] Deed conveying the Property to the Buyer, contingent upon satisfaction of the conditions set forth herein.

5. Fixtures and Improvements. All fixtures, improvements and built-in kitchen and other built-in appliances now in or on the Property that are owned by Seller are included in this sale.

(a) The following items are specifically <u>excluded</u> from the sale: _____

_____

_____

_____.

(b) The following items are specifically <u>included</u> in the sale: _____

_____

_____

_____.

6. Title. At the closing, Seller shall convey marketable title to the Property to Buyer by [Warranty/Quitclaim] Deed, subject only to easements, restrictions, reservations or encumbrances of record acceptable to Buyer in accordance with Section 7, below.

7. Title Insurance. Within thirty (30) days of the date of this Agreement, Buyer shall, at Seller's cost, obtain a commitment for a standard A.L.T.A. owner's policy of title insurance in the amount of the Purchase Price. If the title insurance commitment discloses any matters of title objectionable to Buyer, then Seller may, at Seller's option, cure or obtain insurance over them. If Seller is unable or elects not to cure or obtain necessary insurance over all objectionable exceptions, this Agreement will terminate, the Deposit will be returned to Buyer, and neither party will be obligated further to the other. In the alternative, at Buyer's option, Buyer may elect to accept such title to the Property as Seller is able to provide, without reducing or abating the Purchase Price, without crediting or allowing any sum against the Purchase Price, and without creating any liability in Seller. At the closing, Seller will pay the premium due for the issuance of a policy pursuant to the commitment.

8. Survey. Within five (5) days of the date of this Agreement, Seller will provide Buyer with a copy of any survey of the Property in Seller's possession. Buyer may, at Buyer's option and expense, obtain a new or recertified survey of the Property, as Buyer deems appropriate.

9. Inspections; Buyer Takes "As Is." Within twenty (20) days from the date this Agreement is signed, Buyer may, at Buyer's expense, obtain any inspections of the Property that Buyer desires, including without limitation, inspections of the heating, cooling and ventilation systems, plumbing and electrical systems, and insect and pest infestation. Seller agrees to allow Buyer reasonable access to the Property for the purpose of completing Buyer's inspections. Buyer shall have the right to terminate this Agreement and receive a refund of the Deposit within thirty (30) days from the date of this Agreement if the inspection reports are not acceptable to Buyer by giving Seller written notice (by facsimile or mail). If no such notice is received by Seller within thirty (30) days from the date this Agreement is signed, Buyer shall have been deemed to accept the inspections of the Property.

Buyer agrees that Buyer is not relying on any representation or statement made by Seller or any real estate salesperson regarding any aspect of the Property or this sale transaction, except as may be expressly set forth in this Agreement, a written amendment to this Agreement, or a disclosure statement separately signed by Seller. Accordingly, Buyer agrees to accept the Property "as is" and "with all faults," except as otherwise expressly provided in this Agreement.

10. Contingent Upon Sale of Buyer's Home and Upon Mortgage Financing. It is expressly agreed that Buyer's obligation to complete this transaction is contingent upon the closing on the sale of Buyer's home within sixty (60) days of the execution of this Agreement. Buyer's obligation to close this transaction is also expressly made contingent upon Buyer's ability to obtain a new mortgage upon market rates and terms, at Buyer's option. Seller, at Seller's option, may terminate this Agreement if Buyer has not satisfied or waived this contingency on or before _____, 20____.

11. Contingencies. In addition to any other contingencies set forth herein, the Buyer's obligations under this Agreement are expressly made subject to and contingent upon satisfaction of the following conditions by the time of closing or their waiver by Buyer:

    (a)   Buyer's ability to obtain an enforceable financing commitment from a lender in an amount of not less than ___% of the Purchase Price and on terms satisfactory to Buyer in its sole discretion and close on such financing; and

(b)   Buyer's ability to obtain an appraisal of the Property at an appraised value of not less than the Purchase Price, which is suitable to Buyer and Buyer's lender in their sole discretion; and

(c)   Other contingencies: _____
_____
_____
_____
_____.

In the event that any of these contingencies can not be satisfied, Buyer shall have the right, at any time prior to the closing, to terminate this Agreement and receive a refund of the Deposit.

12. Taxes and Assessments. Seller shall pay all special assessments and real estate taxes levied on the Property in the years prior to closing, including any sidewalk inspection fees or repairs, if required by local ordinances. All special assessments and real estate taxes levied on the Property in the year of closing will be prorated between Buyer and Seller on a calendar year basis, based on the assumption that such taxes are attributable to the calendar year in which they are billed.

13. Closing. The closing shall take place on or before _____, 20___. The closing shall take place at the offices of the title company issuing the commitment for title insurance, or at such other place as the parties may mutually agree.

14. Possession. Buyer shall have possession of the Property immediately after closing.

15. Costs of Closing. Upon delivery of the [Warranty/Quitclaim] Deed to the Property to Buyer, Buyer shall pay for the recording of the deed. Seller shall pay for county and state transfer taxes, if any. Buyer and Seller shall each pay one-half of the fee charged by the title company for closing this transaction.

16. Time of the Essence. Time is of the essence of this Agreement.

17. Disclosure Statements. Seller has delivered to Buyer a Seller's Disclosure Statement as required by Public Act 92 of 1993, and a lead paint disclosure form and booklet, if required.

18. Heirs, Successors and Assigns. This Agreement shall run with the land and shall be binding upon and inure to the benefit of the parties and their respective heirs, successors and assigns, except as otherwise stated herein.

19. Amendment. This Agreement represents the entire agreement between the parties. It may not be amended, altered, or modified unless the party against whom enforcement of any waiver, modification, or discharge is sought does so in writing.

20. Realtor Commission. If either party is responsible to pay any commission, broker's fee, finder's fee, or similar fee on the purchase and sale of this Property, then such fee is the sole responsibility of that party.

21. Condition of the Premises. Buyer's obligation to close is expressly made contingent upon the Premises being in the same condition at the date of closing as it existed on the date of this Agreement, reasonable wear and tear excepted. If any damage should occur prior to closing, all repair and corrective work shall be paid by Seller. In addition, Buyer shall have the right to inspect the Premises immediately prior to the closing in order to determine the satisfaction of this condition.

22. Severability. Except as otherwise provided by this Agreement, the invalidity or unenforceability of any provision of this Agreement will not affect the enforceability or validity of the remaining provisions and this Agreement will be construed in all respects as if such invalid or unenforceable provision were omitted; except, however, that if the invalidity or unenforceability of any provision will affect the basic economic terms of this Agreement or materially affect the rights or obligations of either party, then this Agreement will be deemed terminated.

23. Waiver. No provision of this Agreement may be waived except in a writing signed by both parties. No oral statements, course of conduct, or course of dealing will be deemed to constitute a waiver. No waiver by any party of any breach of this Agreement will be deemed or construed to constitute a waiver of any other breach or as a continuing waiver of any breach.

24. Applicable Law; Construction. This Agreement will be interpreted, construed, enforced, and governed according to the laws of the state of Michigan. Both parties either had professional and legal advice or the opportunity to obtain such advice, and this Agreement is deemed to be mutually drafted.

25. Merger and Modification. This Agreement constitutes the entire agreement between the parties with respect to its subject matter, and all prior discussions, negotiations, and agreements between the parties with respect to such subject matter are deemed merged into this Agreement. No amendment or modification of this Agreement will be enforceable except if in writing and signed by both parties.

26. Survival of Representations and Warranties. All representations and warranties made in this Agreement (if any) shall survive the closing.

27. Notices. Unless otherwise expressly provided for in this Agreement, all notices required or permitted by this Agreement shall be in writing and shall be deemed to be served on the earlier of the date of mailing by first-class mail, postage prepaid, addressed to the other party at the other party's last known address or the date of hand delivery to the other party.

28. Other Terms.

_____

_____

_____.

29. Remedies. In the event of a breach of this Agreement by Seller, Buyer may reclaim its Deposit or sue to specifically enforce the provisions of this Agreement. In the event of a breach of this Agreement by Buyer, Seller's sole remedy shall be to retain the Deposit as liquidated damages, the parties agreeing that it would be difficult or impossible to ascertain Seller's exact damages. The parties agree that for any action brought pursuant to or to enforce any provision of this Agreement, to the extent not otherwise prohibited by law, the prevailing party shall, in addition to any other remedies, be entitled to recover his/her actual costs, including, without limitation, actual reasonable attorneys' fees and other legal expenses incurred to bring, maintain, or defend any such action from its first accrual or notice through any appellate proceedings and collection proceedings.

30. Effective Date. This Agreement shall become effective when executed by all of the parties.

31. Duplicate: This Agreement has been executed in duplicate.

Dated: _____, 20____   _____
                                                                              *

Dated: _____, 20____   _____
                                                                              *
                                                                                                 SELLER

Dated: _____, 20____   _____
                                                                              *

Dated: _____, 20____   _____
                                                                              *
                                                                                                 BUYER

NOTE—This form is just a sample and is for informational purposes only. Prior to entering into a real estate contract, you should consult with a real estate attorney, realtor, real estate broker or other competent professional. This form may have provisions which are not suitable to your transaction, and furthermore, there may be provisions or clauses that would have to be added to or modified in this document to protect your interests.

Attachment D
CHECKLIST FOR PURCHASE/SALES AGREEMENT

1. Preface/introduction.

2. Purchase price.

3. Legal description for the property.

4. Seller's name and address.

5. Buyer's name and address.

6. Financing contingencies.

7. Earnest money/deposit.

8. Escrow issues.

9. Fixtures and items that go with the sale.

10. Land division issues and "split" rights.

11. Type or quality of title to be given.

12. Warranties or "AS-IS" clause.

13. Remedies against default.

14. Title insurance.

15. Closing costs, and who pays what.

16. Property tax proration.

17. Proration of other items (water bill, sewer bill, association dues, etc.).

18. Contingency about flood insurance.

19. General inspections (dwelling, environmental, etc.).

20. "Out" clauses for the buyer (can cancel if not satisfied).

21. Inspections/investigation contingency for "buildability."

22. Miscellaneous contingencies.

23. Dwelling inspections (dwelling, environmental radon, lead paint, etc.).

24. Survey.

25. Real estate transfer taxes.

26. Broker fees/allocations.

27. Possession/occupancy.

28. Closing.

29. Closing date.

30. Place of closing.

31. Seller's disclosure statement (if a dwelling).

32. Lead paint disclosure.

33. Private road disclosure.

34. Type of deed or land contract.

35. Arbitration clause.

36. Sale of existing dwelling contingency.

37. Remedies upon breach or default.

38. Notices.

39. Interpretation/construction clauses.

Attachment E
SELLER DISCLOSURE
STATEMENT
(SAMPLE)

SELLER'S DISCLOSURE STATEMENT

Property Address:_____

_____

Street_____

_____ , Michigan

City, Village, or Township

Purpose of Statement: This statement is a disclosure of the condition of the property in compliance with the Seller Disclosure Act. This statement is a disclosure of the condition and information concerning the property, known by the seller. Unless otherwise advised, the seller does not possess any expertise in construction, architecture, engineering, or any other specific area related to the construction or condition of the improvements on the property or the land. Also, unless otherwise advised, the seller has not conducted any inspection of generally inaccessible areas such as the foundation or roof. This statement is not a warranty of any kind by the seller or by any agent representing the seller in this transaction, and is not a substitute for any inspections or warranties the buyer may wish to obtain.

Seller's Disclosure: The seller discloses the following information with the knowledge that even though this is not a warranty, the seller specifically makes the following representations based on the seller's knowledge at the signing of this document. Upon receiving this statement from the seller, the seller's agent is required to provide a copy to the buyer or the agent of the buyer. The seller authorizes its agent(s) to provide a copy of this statement to any prospective buyer in connection with any actual or anticipated sale of property. The following are representations made solely by the seller and are not the representations of the seller's agent(s), if any. This information is a disclosure only and is not intended to be a part of any contract between buyer and seller.

Instructions to the Seller: (1) Answer ALL questions. (2) Report known conditions affecting the property. (3) Attach additional pages with your signature if additional space is required. (4) Complete this form yourself. (5) If some items do not apply to your property, check NOT AVAILABLE. If you do not know the facts, check UNKNOWN. FAILURE TO PROVIDE A PURCHASER WITH A SIGNED DISCLOSURE STATEMENT WILL ENABLE A PURCHASER TO TERMINATE AN OTHERWISE BINDING PURCHASE AGREEMENT.

Appliances/Systems/Services: The items below are in working order (the items below are included in the sale of the property only if the purchase agreement so provides).

	Yes	No	Unknown	Not Available
Range/oven				
Dishwasher				
Refrigerator				
Hood/fan				
Disposal				
TV antenna, TV rotor & remote control				
Electrical system				
Garage door opener & remote control				
Alarm system				
Intercom				
Central vacuum				
Attic fan				
Pool heater, wall liner & equipment				
Microwave				

	Yes	No	Unknown	Not Available
Trash compactor				
Sauna/hot tub				
Washer				
Dryer				
Lawn sprinkler system				
Water heater				
Plumbing system				
Water softener/conditioner				
Well & pump				
Septic tank & drain field				
Sump pump				
City water system				
City sewer system				
Central air conditioner				
Central heating system				
Wall furnace				
Humidifier				
Electronic air filter				
Solar heating system				
Fireplace & chimney				
Wood burning system				

Explanations (attach additional sheets if necessary):

_____

UNLESS OTHERWISE AGREED, ALL HOUSEHOLD APPLIANCES ARE SOLD IN WORKING ORDER EXCEPT AS NOTED, WITHOUT WARRANTY BEYOND DATE OF CLOSING.

Property conditions, improvements & additional information:

_____

1. Basement/crawl space:
Has there been evidence of water: Yes ❑ No ❑

If yes, please explain:_____
_____.

2. Insulation: Describe if known:_____
_____.

Urea Formaldehyde Foam Insulation (UFFI) is installed?

Unknown ❑   Yes ❑ No ❑

3. Roof: Leaks?   Yes ❑ No ❑

Approximate age if known:_____

4. Well: Type of well (depth/diameter, age, and repair history (if known):
_____
_____.

Has the water been tested?   Yes ❑ No ❑
If yes, date of last report/results:_____
_____.

5. Septic tanks/drain fields: Condition, if known:_____
_____.

6. Heating System: Type/approximate age:_____
_____.

7. Plumbing System: Type: copper ❑ galvanized ❑ other:_____
Any known problems?_____
_____.

8. Electrical System: Any known problems?_____
_____.

9. History of infestation, if any: (termites, carpenter ants, etc.):_____
_____
_____.

10. Environmental Problems: Are you aware of any substances, materials, or products that may be an environmental hazard such as, but not limited to, asbestos, radon gas, formaldehyde, lead-based paint, fuel or chemical storage tanks, and contaminated soil on the property.

Unknown ❑   Yes ❑   No ❑

If yes, please explain:_____
_____.

11. Flood insurance: Do you have flood insurance on the property?

Unknown ❑   Yes ❑ No ❑

12. Mineral rights: Do you own the mineral rights?

Unknown ❑   Yes ❑ No ❑

Other Items: Are you aware of any of the following:

1. Features of the property shared in common with the adjoining landowners, such as walls, fences, roads and driveways, or other features whose use or responsibility for maintenance may have an effect on the property?

Unknown ❏   Yes ❏   No ❏

2. Any encroachments, easements, zoning violations, or nonconforming uses?

Unknown ❏   Yes ❏   No ❏

3. Any "common areas" (facilities like pools, tennis courts, walkways, or other areas co-owned with others), or a homeowners' association that has any authority over the property?

Unknown ❏   Yes ❏   No ❏

4. Structural modifications, alterations, or repairs made without necessary permits or licensed contractors?

Unknown ❏   Yes ❏   No ❏

5. Setting, flooding, drainage, structural, or grading problems?

Unknown ❏   Yes ❏   No ❏

6. Major damage to the property from fire, wind, floods, or landslides?

Unknown ❏   Yes ❏   No ❏

7. Any underground storage tanks?

Unknown ❏   Yes ❏   No ❏

8. Farm or farm operation in the vicinity; or proximity to a landfill, airport, shooting range, etc.?

Unknown ❏   Yes ❏   No ❏

9. Any outstanding utility assessments or fees, including any natural gas main extension surcharge?

Unknown ❏   Yes ❏   No ❏

10. Any outstanding municipal assessments or fees?

Unknown ❏   Yes ❏   No ❏

11. Any pending litigation that could affect the property or the seller's right to convey the property?

Unknown ❏   Yes ❏   No ❏

If the answer to any of these questions is yes, please explain. Attach additional sheets, if necessary: _____
_____
_____
_____.

The seller has lived in the residence on the property from _____ (date) to _____ (date). The seller has owned the property since _____ (date) and makes representation only since that date. The seller has indicated above the condition of all the items based on information known to the seller. If any changes occur in the structural/mechanical/appliance systems of this property from the date of this form to the date of closing, seller will immediately disclose the changes to buyer. In no event shall the parties hold the broker liable for any representations not directly made by the broker or broker's agent.

Seller certifies that the information in this statement is true and correct to the best of seller's knowledge as of the date of seller's signature.

BUYER SHOULD OBTAIN PROFESSIONAL ADVICE AND INSPECTIONS OF THE PROPERTY TO MORE FULLY DETERMINE THE CONDITION OF THE PROPERTY. BUYERS ARE ADVISED THAT CERTAIN INFORMATION COMPILED PURSUANT TO THE SEX OFFENDERS REGISTRATION ACT, 1994 PA 295, MCL 28.721 TO 28.732, IS AVAILABLE TO THE PUBLIC. BUYERS SEEKING THAT INFORMATION SHOULD CONTACT THE APPROPRIATE LOCAL LAW ENFORCEMENT AGENCY OR SHERIFF'S DEPARTMENT DIRECTLY.

BUYER IS ADVISED THAT THE STATE EQUALIZED VALUE OF THE PROPERTY, HOMESTEAD EXEMPTION INFORMATION, AND OTHER REAL PROPERTY TAX INFORMATION IS AVAILABLE FROM THE APPROPRIATE LOCAL ASSESSOR'S OFFICE. BUYER SHOULD NOT ASSUME THAT BUYER'S FUTURE TAX BILLS ON THE PROPERTY WILL BE THE SAME AS THE SELLER'S PRESENT TAX BILLS. UNDER MICHIGAN LAW, REAL PROPERTY TAX OBLIGATIONS CAN CHANGE SIGNIFICANTLY WHEN PROPERTY IS TRANSFERRED.

Seller_____   Date _____
Seller_____   Date _____

Buyer has read and acknowledges receipt of this statement.

Buyer_____   Date _____
                                             Time _____

Buyer_____   Date _____
                                             Time _____

Attachment F
CLOSING CHECKLIST

1. Purchase funds (cashier's check, certified check, or wire transfer).

2. Financing documents:

   (a) Mortgage.

   (b) Land Contract.

3. Seller's closing statement.

4. Buyer's closing statement.

5. Recording fee.

6. State real estate transfer tax.

7. County real estate transfer tax.

8. Proration of property taxes.

9. Proof of identification (usually a driver's license).

10. Real estate transfer affidavit.

11. Homestead exemption form.

12. Estoppel certificate/affidavit.

13. Contingencies met/satisfied acknowledgement.

14. Decide possession date and details.

15. The deed or land contract.

16. HUD forms.

17. Miscellaneous title insurance company forms.

18. Bill of sale (for personal property or non-real estate items).

19. Private road disclosure form.

Attachment G
TITLE INSURANCE COMMITMENT (SAMPLE)

Policy or Policies issued pursuant to this commitment are underwritten by:

First American Title Insurance Company

SCHEDULE A

Commitment No.:   510676
2212   Gary Wadsworth

Date Printed: June 24, 2011

1.   Commitment Date: August 24, 2010 @ 8:00 AM

2.   Policy or Policies to be issued: Policy Amount
     (a) Residential Title Insurance Policy $250,000.00

     Proposed Insured:
     Clifford Bloom, a married man

     Policy or Policies to be issued: Policy Amount
     (b) ALTA Loan Policy (6-17-06)   Without General Exceptions $0.00

     Proposed Insured:

3.   The Fee Simple interest in the land described in this Commitment is owned, at the Commitment Date, by:
     Robert F. Brech Revocable Trust dated 3/31/06

4.   The land referred to in this Commitment, situated in the County of Lake, Township of Webber, State of Michigan,
     is described as follows:

     Lot(s) 32, 33 and 90, Plat of Lazy Acres, according to the recorded plat thereof, as recorded in Liber 2 of Plats,
     Page 47.

5706 S. Lazy Deer Lane Baldwin MI

Issued By: First American Title Insurance Company
For questions regarding this commitment contact;
(616)975-4102 or fax to (866)416-9827
5730 Eagle Drive Southeast
Grand Rapids, MI 49512

First American Title Insurance Company
5730 Eagle Drive Southeast
Grand Rapids, MI 49512

Schedule B – Section I
REQUIREMENTS

Commitment No.: 510676

General Requirements

The following requirements must be met:

(a)   Payment of the full consideration to, or for the account of, the grantors or mortgagors should be made.

(b)   Payment of all taxes, charges, assessments, levied and assessed against subject premises, which are due and payable should be made.

(c)   Pay us the premiums, fees and charges for the policy.

(d)   You must tell us in writing the name of anyone not referred to in this Commitment who will receive an interest in the land or who will make a loan on the land. We may make additional requirements or exceptions.

(e)   Submit completed Owner's Estoppel/Affidavit/ALTA Statement on the form provided by this company and signed by or on behalf of all owners.

Specific Requirements

Documents satisfactory to us creating the interest in the land and/or mortgage to be insured must be signed, delivered and recorded:

1.   A CERTIFICATE OF TRUST IN ACCORDANCE WITH MCL 565.432, WHICH CERTIFIES THE FOLLOWING:

     A)   Name or Title of Trust,

     B)   Date of Trust Agreement and Amendments thereto,

     C)   Names and addresses of all Trustees and Successor Trustees,

     D)   Legal description of the affected real property, and

     E)   Verbatim reproductions of provisions in the Trust Agreement and Amendments thereto regarding:

         1) The powers of the Trustee(s) relating to real property and restrictions on the powers of the Trustee(s) relating to real property;

         2) The governing law; and

         3) Amendment of the Trust relating to Trust provisions, certificate that the Trust Agreement remains in full force and effect, and a list of the names and addresses of all persons who at the time the certificate is executed are Trustees of the Trust.

     SAID CERTIFICATE MUST BE EXECUTED BY ONE OF THE FOLLOWING:

     A)   The Settlor or Grantor of the Trust,

     B)   An attorney for the Settlor, Grantor or the Trustee,

     C)   An officer of a banking institution acting as Trustee, or

     D)   An attorney acting as Trustee.

3.   WARRANTY DEED FROM CURRENT TRUSTEE(S) OF ROBERT F. BRECHTING REVOCABLE TRUST DATED 7/31/06 TO CLIFFORD BLOOM, A MARRIED MAN

4.   PROVIDE SATISFACTORY EVIDENCE THAT THE SUBJECT PROPERTY IS NOT SUBJECT TO ANY LIEN IN FAVOR OF A HOMEOWNER'S ASSOCIATION FOR UNPAID DUES OR ASSESSMENTS.

     NOTE: Attention is directed to Section 261 of Public Act 591 of 1996, being the Land Division Act, which states in part "No Person shall sell any lot in a recorded plat or any parcel of unplatted land in an unincorporated area if it abuts a street or road which has not been accepted as public unless the seller first informs the purchaser in writing on a separate instrument to be attached to the instrument conveying any interest in such lot or parcel of land of the fact that the street or road is private and is not required to be maintained by the board of county road commissioners".

4.   Pay unpaid taxes and assessments unless shown as paid:
              2010 Summer Taxes in the amount of $581.39 are DUE
              2009 Winter Taxes in the amount of $1677.64 are PAID
              Tax Parcel Identification:
                     Property Address: 5706 S. Lazy Deer Lane
                     Tax Parcel No.: 43-11-560-032-01
                     2010 State Equalized Value: $66,100
                     2010 Taxable Value: $47,813
                     Principal Residence Exemption, as of past December 31: 0%
              Special Assessments: unavailable

              School District: BALDWIN

The amounts shown as due do not include collection fees, penalties or interest.

NOTE: If subject property is connected to public/community water or sewer, furnish a copy of the current bill showing that all charges have been paid to date or the Owner's Policy to be issued will include an exception on Schedule B for water and sewer charges which became a lien prior to the date of the Policy.

First American Title Insurance Company
5730 Eagle Drive Southeast
Grand Rapids, MI 49512

Schedule B – Section II
EXCEPTIONS

Commitment No.: 510676

Schedule B of the policy or policies to be issued will contain exceptions to the following matters unless the same are disposed of to the satisfaction of the Company:

Defects, liens encumbrances adverse claims or other matters, if any, created, first appearing in the public records or attaching subsequent to the effective date hereof but prior to the date the Proposed Insured acquires for value of record the estate or interest or mortgage thereon covered by this Commitment.

Part One: General Exceptions
Any policy we issue will have the following exceptions unless they are taken care of to our satisfaction:

1. Rights or claims of parties in possession not shown by the public records.
2. Encroachments, overlaps, boundary line disputes, or other matters which would be disclosed by an accurate survey and inspection of the premises.
3. Easements, or claims of easements, not shown by the public records.
4. Any lien, or right to a lien, for services, labor or material heretofore or hereafter furnished, imposed by law and not shown on the public records.
5. Taxes or special assessments which are not shown as existing liens by the public records.

Part Two: Specific Exceptions

1.   Covenants, conditions, restrictions and other provisions but omitting restrictions, if any, based on race, color, religion, sex, handicap, familial status or national origin as contained in instrument recorded in Liber 309, page 24.

2.   Easement(s) as disclosed by the recorded plat, if any.

3.   Rights of the United States, State of Michigan and the public for commerce, navigation, recreation and fishery, in any portion of the land comprising the bed of Little Star Lake, or land created by fill or artificial accretion.

4.   The nature, extent or lack of riparian rights or the riparian rights of riparian owners and the public in and to the use of the waters of Little Star Lake.

     NOTE: Streets and roads in platted subdivision are dedicated to the use of the Lot owners.

5.   Interest of others in oil, gas and mineral rights, if any, recorded in the public records or unrecorded.

     NOTE: Access to the land is by means of a private road that is not maintained by the County Road Commission.

6.   Lien for outstanding water or sewer charges, if any.

Commitment for Title Insurance
FIRST AMERICAN TITLE INSURANCE COMPANY.

First American Title Insurance Company, a California corporation ("Company"), for a valuable consideration, commits to issue its policy or policies of title insurance, as identified in Schedule A, in favor of the Proposed Insured named in Schedule A, as owner or mortgagee of the estate or interest in the land described or referred to in Schedule A, upon payment of the premiums and charges and compliance with the Requirements; all subject to the provisions of Schedules A and B and to the Conditions of this Commitment.

This Commitment shall be effective only when the identity of the Proposed Insured and the amount of the policy or policies committed for have been inserted in Schedule A by the Company.

All liability and obligation under this Commitment shall cease and terminate six (6) months after the effective Date or when the policy or policies committed for shall issue, whichever first occurs, provided that the failure to issue the policy or policies is not the fault of the Company.

The Company will provide a sample of the policy form upon request.

First American Title Insurance Company

Dennis J. Gilmore
President

Timothy Kemp
Secretary

CONDITIONS:

1. The term mortgage, when used herein, shall include deed of trust, trust deed, or other security instrument.

2. If the proposed Insured has or acquired actual knowledge of any defect, lien, encumbrance, adverse claim of other matter affecting the estate or interest or mortgage thereon covered by this Commitment other than those shown in Schedule B hereof, and shall fail to disclose such knowledge to the Company in writing, the Company shall be relieved from liability for any loss or damage resulting from any act of reliance hereon to the extent the Company is prejudiced by failure to so disclose such knowledge. If the proposed Insured shall disclose such knowledge to the Company, or if the Company otherwise acquires actual knowledge of any such defect, lien, encumbrance, adverse claim or other matter, the Company at its option may amend Schedule B of this Commitment accordingly, but such amendment shall not relieve the Company from liability previously incurred pursuant to paragraph 3 of these Conditions and Stipulations.

3. Liability of the Company under this Commitment shall be only to the named proposed Insured and such parties included under the definition of Insured in the form of policy or policies committed for and only for actual loss incurred in reliance hereon in undertaking in good faith (a) to comply with the requirements hereof, or (b) to eliminate exceptions shown in Schedule B, or (c) to acquire or create the estate or interest or mortgage thereon covered by this Commitment. In no event shall such liability exceed the amount stated in Schedule A for the policy or policies committed for and such liability is subject to the insuring provisions and Conditions and Stipulations and the Exclusions from Coverage of the form of policy or policies committed for in favor of the proposed Insured which are hereby incorporated by reference and are made a part of this Commitment except as expressly modified herein.

4. This Commitment is a contract to issue one or more title insurance policies and is not an abstract of title or a report of the condition of title. Any action or actions or rights of action that the proposed Insured may have or may bring against the Company arising out of the status of the title to the estate or interest or the status of the mortgage thereon covered by this Commitment must be based on and are subject to the provisions of this Commitment.

5. The policy to be issued contains an arbitration clause. All arbitrable matters when the Amount of Insurance is $2,000,000 or less shall be arbitrated at the option of either the Company or the Insured as the exclusive remedy of the parties. You may review a copy of the arbitration rules at http://www.alta.org/.

Issued by: **First American Title Insurance Company**
5730 Eagle Drive Southeast
Grand Rapids, Michigan 49512
Ph: (616)975-4102 or Fax to: (866)416-9827

First American Title

Privacy Information
We Are Committed to Safeguarding Customer Information
In order to better serve your needs now and in the future, we may ask you to provide us with certain information. We understand that you may be concerned about what we will do with such information - particularly any personal or financial information. We agree that you have a right to know how we will utilize the personal information you provide to us. Therefore, together with our subsidiaries we have adopted this Privacy Policy to govern the use and handling of your personal information.

Applicability
This Privacy Policy governs our use of the information that you provide to us. It does not govern the manner in which we may use information we have obtained from any other source, such as information obtained from a public record or from another person or entity. First American has also adopted broader guidelines that govern our use of personal information regardless of its source. First American calls these guidelines its Fair Information Values.

Types of Information
Depending upon which of our services you are utilizing, the types of nonpublic personal information that we may collect include:
- Information we receive from you on applications, forms and in other communications to us, whether in writing, in person, by telephone or any other means;
- Information about your transactions with us, our affiliated companies, or others; and
- Information we receive from a consumer reporting agency.

Use of Information
We request information from you for our own legitimate business purposes and not for the benefit of any nonaffiliated party. Therefore, we will not release your information to nonaffiliated parties except: (1) as necessary for us to provide the product or service you have requested of us; or (2) as permitted by law. We may, however, store such information indefinitely, including the period after which any customer relationship has ceased. Such information may be used for any internal purpose, such as quality control efforts or customer analysis. We may also provide all of the types of nonpublic personal information listed above to one or more of our affiliated companies. Such affiliated companies include financial service providers, such as title insurers, property and casualty insurers, and trust and investment advisory companies, or companies involved in real estate services, such as appraisal companies, home warranty companies and escrow companies. Furthermore, we may also provide all the information we collect, as described above, to companies that perform marketing services on our behalf, on behalf of our affiliated companies or to other financial institutions with whom we or our affiliated companies have joint marketing agreements.

Former Customers
Even if you are no longer our customer, our Privacy Policy will continue to apply to you.

Confidentiality and Security
We will use our best efforts to ensure that no unauthorized parties have access to any of your information. We restrict access to nonpublic personal information about you to those individuals and entities who need to know that information to provide products or services to you. We will use our best efforts to train and oversee our employees and agents to ensure that your information will be handled responsibly and in accordance with this Privacy Policy and First American's Fair Information Values. We currently maintain physical, electronic, and procedural safeguards that comply with federal regulations to guard your nonpublic personal information.

Information Obtained Through Our Web Site
First American Financial Corporation is sensitive to privacy issues on the Internet. We believe it is important you know how we treat the information about you we receive on the Internet.
In general, you can visit First American or its affiliates' Web sites on the World Wide Web without telling us who you are or revealing any information about yourself. Our Web servers collect the domain names, not the e-mail addresses, of visitors. This information is aggregated to measure the number of visits, average time spent on the site, pages viewed and similar information. First American uses this information to measure the use of our site and to develop ideas to improve the content of our site.
There are times, however, when we may need information from you, such as your name and email address. When information is needed, we will use our best efforts to let you know at the time of collection how we will use the personal information. Usually, the personal information we collect is used only by us to respond to your inquiry, process an order or allow you to access specific account/profile information. If you choose to share any personal information with us, we will only use it in accordance with the policies outlined above.

Business Relationships
First American Financial Corporation's site and its affiliates' sites may contain links to other Web sites. While we try to link only to sites that share our high standards and respect for privacy, we are not responsible for the content or the privacy practices employed by other sites.

Cookies
Some of First American's Web sites may make use of "cookie" technology to measure site activity and to customize information to your personal tastes. A cookie is an element of data that a Web site can send to your browser, which may then store the cookie on your hard drive.
FirstAm.com uses stored cookies. The goal of this technology is to better serve you when visiting our site, save you time when you are here and to provide you with a more meaningful and productive Web site experience.

Fair Information Values
Fairness We consider consumer expectations about their privacy in all our businesses. We only offer products and services that assure a favorable balance between consumer benefits and consumer privacy.
Public Record We believe that an open public record creates significant value for society, enhances consumer choice and creates consumer opportunity. We actively support an open public record and emphasize its importance and contribution to our economy.
Use We believe we should behave responsibly when we use information about a consumer in our business. We will obey the laws governing the collection, use and dissemination of data.
Accuracy We will take reasonable steps to help assure the accuracy of the data we collect, use and disseminate. Where possible, we will take reasonable steps to correct inaccurate information. When, as with the public record, we cannot correct inaccurate information, we will take all reasonable steps to assist consumers in identifying the source of the erroneous data so that the consumer can secure the required corrections.
Education We endeavor to educate the users of our products and services, our employees and others in our industry about the importance of consumer privacy. We will instruct our employees on our fair information values and on the responsible collection and use of data. We will encourage others in our industry to collect and use information in a responsible manner.
Security We will maintain appropriate facilities and systems to protect against unauthorized access to and corruption of the data we maintain.

This sample title insurance commitment is provided courtesy of First American Title Insurance Company and has been reprinted with its permission. First American Title Insurance Company is pleased to provide a variety of different services regarding real estate matters throughout Michigan.

Attachment H
WARRANTY DEED
(SAMPLE)

WARRANTY DEED

THE GRANTOR: _____
[Followed by: "husband and wife" or "a married man" or
"a single man" or no designation if grantor is a single or
married woman owning solely. The grantor may also be
a trust or other entity. If the grantor is a married man,
then a dower waiver is also required as shown below.]

WHOSE ADDRESS IS:_____

CONVEYS AND WARRANTS

TO THE GRANTEE:_____

WHOSE ADDRESS IS:_____

the real estate situated in the City/Township/Village of
_____, _____ County,
Michigan, more fully described on **Exhibit A** as attached to this Deed
(the "Premises"), together with all improvements, fixtures, easements,
hereditaments and appurtenances associated with the Premises, but
subject to easements, restrictions and reservations of record.

Grantor grants to Grantee the right to make [all/zero/number] divisions under the Michigan Land Division Act. This Property may be located within the vicinity of farmland or a farm operation. Generally accepted agriculture and management practices which may generate noise, dust, odors, and other associated conditions may be used and are protected by the Michigan Right to Farm Act.

For consideration of $_____.

Dated: _____, 20___

[Name of Grantor if entity]

_____

[Printed name of Grantor (and capacity if Grantor is an entity)]

_____

[Printed name of Grantor (and capacity if Grantor is an entity)]

_____

ACKNOWLEDGEMENT

STATE OF MICHIGAN)
) ss.
COUNTY OF   )

Acknowledged before me in _____ County, Michigan on _____, 20___, by _____ **["husband and wife" or "a married man" or "a single man" or none if a single or married woman]** who is personally known to me or who has produced [his/her/their] Michigan driver's license as identification.

Notary Public, _____ County, Michigan
Acting in _____ County
My commission expires: _____

[Where the Grantor is a married man, then his wife must also sign to waive her dower interest by adding following after the signature block and substituting the following notary:]

_____, a married woman, signs below for the sole purpose of extinguishing her dower interest, if any, in and to the Premises.

Dated: _____, 20___ By_____,
a married woman

STATE OF MICHIGAN)
) ss.
COUNTY OF   )

Acknowledged before me in _____ County, Michigan on
_____, 20___, by _____, a
married man and _____, his wife, who are
personally known to me or who have produced their Michigan driver's
licenses as identification.

                   Notary Public, _____ County, Michigan
                   Acting in _____ County
                   My commission expires: _____

[If the Grantor is an entity, then a different form of notary specific to the entity may be required. In general, the name of the Grantor, the capacity of the signatory, and the type of the entity will be recited.]

DRAFTED BY AND WHEN

RECORDED RETURN TO:

[Name of Drafter]

[Address of Drafter]

EXHIBIT A

LEGAL DESCRIPTION

Real property situated in the City/Village/Township of _____,
_____ County, Michigan, legally described as:

_____
_____
_____
_____

_____

Permanent Parcel No. _____

_____
_____
_____
_____
_____
_____

* * *

NOTE—This form is just a sample and is for informational purposes only. Prior to using a real estate document, you should consult with a real estate attorney, realtor, real estate broker, or other competent professional. This form may have provisions which are not suitable to your transaction, and furthermore, there may be provisions or clauses that would have to be added to or modified in this document to protect your interests.

Attachment I
QUITCLAIM DEED
(SAMPLE)

QUITCLAIM DEED

GRANTOR: _____

_____

WHOSE ADDRESS IS: _____

_____ ("Grantor")

QUITCLAIMS TO GRANTEE: _____

WHOSE ADDRESS IS: _____

_____ (Grantee")

The land and rights located within [City/Village/Township], _____ County, Michigan, more particularly legally and otherwise described on Exhibit A as attached hereto.

For consideration of less than $100.00.

Grantor grants to Grantee the right to make [all/zero/number] land divisions pursuant to the Michigan Land Division Act, being MCL 560.101 *et seq.*

The premises may be located within the vicinity of farmland or a farm operation. Generally accepted agriculture and management practices which may generate noise, dust, odors, and other associated conditions may be used and are protected by the Michigan Right to Farm Act.

This transaction is exempt from state and county transfer tax pursuant to MCL 207.526(a) and 207.505(a).

By _____

STATE OF MICHIGAN)
) ss.
COUNTY OF   )

The foregoing was acknowledged before me this _____ day of _____, 20____, by _____, who is personally known to me or who has produced his/her Michigan driver's license as identification.

Notary Public, _____ County, Michigan
Acting in _____ County
My commission expires: _____

DRAFTED BY AND WHEN RECORDED RETURN TO:

_____

_____

_____

_____

EXHIBIT A

Legal Description

_____

_____

_____

_____

_____

_____

_____

Permanent Parcel Number _____

Common Address _____

* * *

NOTE—This form is just a sample and is for informational purposes only. Prior to entering into any real estate document, you should consult with a real estate attorney, realtor, real estate broker, or other competent professional. This form may have provisions which are not suitable to your transaction and furthermore, there may be provisions or clauses that would have to be added to or modified in this document to protect your interests.

Attachment J
LAND CONTRACT
(SAMPLE)

LAND CONTRACT

This Land Contract (the "Contract"), is entered into on this _____ day of_____, 20___, between _____ _____, of _____ _____ ("Seller") and _____ _____ of ___ _____ _____ ("Buyer") pursuant to the following terms and conditions:

1. Description of Premises. Seller agrees to sell and convey to Buyer land in the City/Village/Township of _____, _____ County, Michigan, with a street address of _____ _____, a Permanent Parcel Number of _____, and legally described as:

[INSERT PROPERTY LEGAL DESCRIPTION]

together with all improvements, buildings, fixtures, appurtenances, tenements and hereditaments (the "Premises") on the Premises as of this date; but subject to easements and restrictions of record and zoning laws and ordinances affecting the Premises.

2. Price, Interest, and Terms. Buyer agrees to purchase the Premises from Seller, and to pay to Seller a purchase price of _____

Dollars ($_____), of which the sum of _____
Dollars ($_____) has already been paid to Seller. Buyer agrees
to pay to Seller the balance of _____ Dollars
($_____) together with interest on any principal from time to time
unpaid, in the following manner: _____

_____

_____

_____

_____.

The interest mentioned above shall be at a rate of _____
percent (_____%) per year, from _____, 20___,
computed _____ and first deducted from each payment with
the remainder applied to principal. Each payment of principal and interest
not paid when due shall be assessed a one-time charge of five percent
(5%), and in addition shall also bear interest upon the interest portion of
the payment until paid at the above stated contract interest rate but not
to exceed ten percent (10%). Both the late charge and the interest upon
interest shall be separate amounts owed under this contract and shall
be due and payable immediately upon the occurrence of the default. All
payments shall be made at _____,
or wherever otherwise directed by Seller in writing.

3. Possession. Buyer shall receive possession of the Premises on
_____, 20___, but after the closing, and shall be
entitled to retain possession only so long as there is no default by Buyer
in carrying out the terms and conditions of this Contract. Possession is
also subject to the following rights of any tenants in possession: _____

_____

_____

_____

_____.

4. Buyer's Duties.

Buyer agrees:

   (a) To purchase the Premises and pay Seller the sum aforesaid, with
        interest thereon as above provided.

   (b) To use, maintain, and occupy the Premises in accordance with any
        and all zoning, building, and use restrictions applicable thereto.

   (c) To keep the Premises in compliance with all police, fire, sanitary,
        or other regulations and codes imposed by any governmental
        authority.

(d) To keep and maintain the Premises and the buildings, fixtures, and structures in as good condition as they are at the date hereof and not to commit waste, remove, or demolish any improvements thereon, or otherwise diminish the value of Seller's security, without the written consent of Seller.

(e) To pay all taxes and special assessments hereafter levied on the Premises before any penalty for non-payment attaches thereto, and submit receipts to Seller upon request, as evidence of payment thereof; and also at all times to keep the buildings, fixtures, and structures now or hereafter on the land insured against loss and damage.

5. Insurance. Buyer shall obtain and keep in force at all times fire and extended coverage insurance in the name of Seller covering the buildings and improvements now or hereafter placed on the Premises with a loss payable clause or other endorsement making the proceeds payable to Seller and Buyer as their respective interests may appear, with insurers satisfactory to Seller in an amount not less than the insurable value of the Premises, and shall deliver copies of the insurance policies to Seller with premium paid.

6. Disposition of Insurance Proceeds. In case of loss of damage as a result of which insurance proceeds are available in an amount sufficient to repair or rebuild the Premises, Buyer has the right to elect to use the insurance proceeds to repair or rebuild. In order to elect to exercise the right, Buyer must give Seller written notice of the election within 60 days of the loss or damage. If the election is made, the insurance proceeds shall be used for that purpose. In the event the insurance proceeds are not sufficient to repair or rebuild the Premises, Buyer may elect to use the proceeds to repair or rebuild by giving written notice of the election within 60 days of the loss of damage, and along with the notice, deposit with Seller an amount sufficient to provide for full payment of the repair and rebuilding. If the election, and deposit if required, are not timely made, the insurance proceeds shall be applied on this Contract. If the insurance proceeds exceed the amount required for repairing and rebuilding, the excess shall be applied first toward the satisfaction of any existing defaults under the terms of this Contract, and then as a prepayment upon the principal balance owing, without penalty, notwithstanding any other provision to the contrary. The prepayment shall not defer the time for payment of any remaining payments under Paragraph 2 of this Contract. Any surplus of proceeds in excess of the balance owing on this Contract, shall be paid to Buyer.

7. Insurance and/or Tax Default. In case of failure of Buyer to obtain, maintain, or deliver policies of insurance or to pay taxes or special assessments payable by Buyer, Seller may (at Seller's option):

(a) Pay the insurance premiums, taxes, or special assessments and add them to the unpaid balance on the contract, or

(b) Pay the insurance premiums, taxes, or special assessments and treat Buyer's failure to pay them as a default, or

(c) Not pay the insurance premiums, taxes, or special assessments and treat Buyer's failure to pay them as a default.

8. Taxes. Buyer shall pay all taxes and special assessments upon the Premises which shall become due and payable after the date of this Contract before they become subject to penalties, and shall produce evidence of the payment to Seller on demand.

Other tax provisions: _____
_____
_____.

9. Waste. Buyer shall at all times maintain the Premises in the same condition it was in on the date of possession, reasonable wear and tear excepted, and Buyer shall not commit or suffer any other person to commit waste or, without the consent of Seller in writing, remove, change, or demolish the improvements on the Premises in a way which may diminish Seller's security.

10. Seller's Right to Mortgage. Seller's right to place a mortgage on the Premises, or renew or amend any existing mortgage, is subject to the following limitations:

(a) The aggregate amount due on all outstanding mortgages shall not, at any time, be greater than the unpaid principal of this Contract;

(b) The aggregate payments of principal and interest required in any one year under the new or renewal mortgage or mortgages shall not exceed those required under this Contract;

(c) The mortgage or mortgages shall not be amended to extend the term beyond the length of this Contract;

(d) Seller shall give to Buyer written notice of the execution of any mortgage or renewal, containing the name and address of the mortgagee, the amount and rate of interest on the mortgage, the due date of payments and maturity of the principal;

(e) Seller covenants to meet the payments of principal and interest as they mature on any mortgage now or hereafter placed upon the Premises and produce evidence of payment to Buyer on demand; and

(f) In case Seller shall default upon any mortgage, Buyer shall have the right to do the acts or make the payments necessary to cure the default and shall be reimbursed by receiving credit to apply on the payments due or to become due on this Contract.

When the Contract payments have reduced the amount due to the amount of the mortgage indebtedness, Buyer shall be entitled to demand and receive the deed hereinafter mentioned, subject to the mortgage indebtedness which Buyer shall assume and agree to pay; provided that the mortgage by its terms does not prohibit assumption.

11. Seller to Perform any Prior Land Contract(s). If, at the time this Contract is executed, Seller is purchasing the Premises on a land contract or contracts, Seller covenants and agrees to meet all obligations of such contract(s) as they mature and produce evidence thereof to Buyers on demand. If Seller shall default on any prior land contract obligations, Buyer may cure the default and any payments by Buyer shall be credited on the sums first due on this Contract.

Whenever the sum due and owing on this Contract is reduced to the amount owing upon the prior land contract(s) by which Seller is purchasing the Premises, and if Buyer is not in default, Buyer shall be entitled to demand and receive an assignment of Seller's right, title, and interest in and to the prior land contract(s), provided that Buyer shall assume and pay the prior land contract(s), and provided further that the prior land contract(s) does not prohibit assignment.

12. Enforcement on Default; Acceleration. If Buyer shall fail to perform any of the covenants of conditions contained in this Contract on or before the date on which the performance is required, Seller may:

(a) Give Buyer a written notice specifying the default and informing Buyer that if the default continues for a period of fifteen (15) days after service of the notice that Seller will without further notice declare the entire balance due and payable, and proceed according to the common law or the statutes of the state of Michigan; or

(b) Not declare the entire balance due and payable, and proceed according to the common law or the statutes of the state of Michigan including but not limited to the right of Seller to declare a forfeiture in consequence of the nonpayment of any money required to be paid under the Contract or any other breach of the Contract, but in the event Seller elects to proceed under the sub-paragraph then Seller shall give Buyer a written notice of forfeiture specifying the default which has occurred and shall give Buyer a period of fifteen days after service of the notice of forfeiture to cure the default.

13. Assignment. Either party may assign, sell, or convey an interest in this Contract, but shall immediately give written notice to the other party of the action, which notice shall give the name and address of the new party.

No assignment, sale, or conveyance shall release Buyer from Buyer's obligations under the provisions of this Contract unless Seller expressly releases Buyer in writing.

14. Buyer's Acceptance of Title and Premises. Buyer acknowledges having been previously advised to request an attorney at law to examine either:

(a) An abstract of title and tax history of the Premises certified to _____

_____

_____; or

(b) A policy of title insurance or binder covering the Premises, dated

_____;

and agrees to accept as merchantable the title now disclosed thereby except: _____

_____

_____

_____.

15. Seller's Duty of Conveyance. Upon full final payment of the principal and interest of this Contract within the time and the manner required by this Contract, together with all other sums chargeable against Buyer, and upon full performance of the covenants and agreements of Buyer, Seller shall promptly convey the Premises to Buyer or Buyer's legal representative, successors or assigns by [Warranty/Quitclaim] Deed, subject to easements and restrictions of record and free from all other encumbrances except those, if any, as shall have been expressly assumed by Buyer and except those, if any, as shall have arisen through the acts of neglect of Buyer or others holding through Buyer. At the time of delivery of the deed, Seller will deliver all insurance policies mentioned in this Contract properly assigned by Seller to Buyer, and at Seller's expense either an abstract of title certified from the date of purchase under this Contract to a date within thirty (30) days of the date of the deed or, in the event a policy of title insurance has previously been furnished, then a title search to a date within thirty (30) days of the date of the deed.

16. Termination. The term of this Contract shall terminate upon the date the last payment is due as set forth in Paragraph 2 unless it shall sooner be terminated by its terms.

17. Loan of Papers. Upon request, Seller shall deliver the abstract or the policy of title insurance or binder to Buyer for a period not exceeding thirty (30) days, for which Buyer shall give a receipt.

18. Recording. The parties hereto agree that only the following shall be recorded with the County Register of Deeds:

_____ An original of this Contract, or

_____ A Memorandum of Land Contract

19. No Warranties or Representations. Except for any title warranties or other guarantees expressly specified in this Contract, Buyer takes the Premises "AS-IS" and in its current condition.

20. Service of Notices. Any and all notices or demands shall be sufficient when served as follows:

(a) By personal service on the party or to a member of the party's family or employee of suitable age and discretion with a request that the notice or demand be personally delivered to the party; or

(b) By depositing the notice or demand in the United States Post Office with postage fully prepaid by first-class mail, addressed to the party at the party's last known address.

21. Time of Essence; Waiver. It is expressly understood and agreed that time shall be deemed of the essence of this Contract. Failure of Seller to exercise any right upon default of Buyer shall not constitute a waiver of any rights and shall not prevent Seller from exercising any of Seller's rights upon subsequent default.

22. Capacity of Parties. The individual parties hereto represent themselves to be of full age. Any corporate parties hereto represent themselves to be existing corporations with their charter or the equivalent in full force and effect. Any partnership parties hereto represent themselves to be existing partnerships with their certificates or the equivalent in full force and effect. The parties hereto represent that they have full authority to enter into this Contract and to make it fully binding.

23. Additional Items Included. The following additional items on the Premises are also included with this Contract: _____

24. Remedies. Both parties shall have such remedies to enforce or for violation of this Contract as are allowed by Michigan law and equity.

25. Additional Provisions. _____

_____

_____

_____

_____

_____

_____.

26. Binding Effect. The covenants and agreements of this Contract shall run with the land and shall also bind the heirs, assigns, and successors of the respective parties.

27. Modification. This Contract shall not be altered, modified or varied except in a writing signed by both parties.

28. Effective Date. The parties have signed this Contract in duplicate and it shall be effective as of the day and year first above written.

SELLER:

* _____

* _____

STATE OF MICHIGAN)
) ss.
COUNTY OF   )

The foregoing was acknowledged before me this _____ day of _____, 20____, by _____ and _____, who are personally known to me or who have produced their Michigan driver's licenses as identification.

Notary Public, _____ County, Michigan
Acting in _____ County
My commission expires: _____

BUYER:

* _____

* _____

STATE OF MICHIGAN)
) ss.
COUNTY OF   )

The foregoing was acknowledged before me this _____ day of
_____, 20_____ by _____ and
_____, who are personally known to me or who
have produced their Michigan driver's licenses as identification.

                            Notary Public, _____ County, Michigan
                            Acting in _____ County
                            My commission expires: _____

This instrument drafted by
and when recorded return to:

[DRAFTER NAME]

[DRAFTER ADDRESS]

* * *

NOTE—This form is just a sample and is for informational purposes
only. Prior to entering into a land contract, you should consult with
a real estate attorney, realtor, real estate broker, or other competent
professional. This form may have provisions which are not suitable to
your transaction, and furthermore, there may be provisions or clauses
that would have to be added to or modified in this document to protect
your interests.

Attachment K
CHECKLIST FOR POTENTIAL OBSTACLES TO BUILDING A DWELLING ON A LAKEFRONT LOT
(or Expanding or Replacing an Existing Dwelling) or Installing a Seawall, Dock, Raft, Etc.

1. <u>Dwellings, generally:</u>

   (a) Local municipal (city, village, township, or county) zoning ordinance.

   (b) Local municipal (city, village, township, or county) general ordinances and codes.

   (c) The presence of a floodplain (regulated by federal law, and sometimes, by local municipal ordinance), flooding, etc.

   (d) The ability to fill or alter wetlands without a permit (generally covered by the Michigan Department of Natural Resources and the Environment in most cases, although, on occasion, the U.S. Army Corps of Engineers has co-equal jurisdiction with the DNRE on the Great Lakes and along certain rivers, while a few local municipalities have their own additional wetlands protection ordinances).

   (e) The Michigan Dune Protection Act.

   (f) The Michigan Natural Rivers Act (administered through the DNRE, although local municipalities often have their own additional river protection ordinances).

   (g) Permits for building lakeward of the ordinary high water mark on the Great Lakes (typically governed by both the DNRE and the U.S. Army Corps of Engineers).

(h) Permits for building lakeward of the ordinary high water mark on inland lakes (typically governed by both the DNRE, but on a few lakes connected to the Great Lakes, the U.S. Army Corps of Engineers has concurrent jurisdiction).

(i) Local municipal ordinances that limit placing dwellings or other buildings on steep slopes.

(j) County health department regulations or local municipal ordinances that prohibit installing a dwelling or other accessory buildings where the water table is located close to the surface of the ground.

(k) If within 500 feet of a lake or other body of water and ground disturbance reaches a certain minimum threshold, must obtain a Michigan soil and sedimentation permit from the local road commission, county drain commissioner, or other agency administering the statute.

(l) If a private well or septic system is required, county health department or other applicable agency permits/approval.

(m) Utilities to the site.

(n) Access (private road ordinances, steep slopes, drive cut permit, etc.).

(o) Building codes.

(p) Soil erosion and sedimentation permit.

2. Installing seawalls, altering the shoreline of a lake or river, or dredging.

(a) The Michigan Wetland Protection Act (as well as potentially local municipal ordinances) may be an issue.

(b) No seawall can be installed, no dredging, fill, or alteration can occur lakeside of the ordinary high water mark on inland lakes in Michigan without obtaining a DNRE permit pursuant to what used to be called the "Inland Lakes and Streams Act" (MCL 324.30101 *et seq.*).

(c) The Michigan Dune Protection Act.

(d) On the Great Lakes, will likely need approval from the U.S. Army Corps of Engineers under federal law, as well as DNRE approval under MCL 324.32501.

3. Installing a dock.

(a) May be subject to local zoning or police power ordinance provisions.

(b) No permanent dock can be installed without a DNRE permit pursuant to MCL 324.30101 *et seq.*

(c) If a dock poses a hazard to navigation, the DNRE can require it to be removed or shortened pursuant to MCL 324.80163.

(d) If two or more families utilize a common dock, it is deemed a "marina" for which a DNRE permit must be obtained pursuant to MCL 324.30101 *et seq.* In addition, such usage might violate the single-family residential regulations of the local municipal zoning ordinance.

(e) On the Great Lakes, will likely need approval by the U.S. Army Corps of Engineers under federal law, as well as potentially approval by the DNRE pursuant to MCL 324.32501.

(f) On certain inland lakes connected to the Great Lakes, will likely need approval by the U.S. Army Corps of Engineers under federal law, as well as potentially approval by the DNRE pursuant to MCL 324.32501.

4.   Rafts, floating trampolines, etc.

(a) May be subject to a local municipal ordinance.

(b) If the raft is a hazard to navigation, the DNRE can require that it be removed from the body of water or moved pursuant to MCL 324.80163.

5.   Swim buoys in inland lake.

(a) May need a permit from the DNRE under MCL 324.80159 *et seq.*

6.   Boat ramps.

(a) Will likely need a permit from the DNRE to install, expand, or modify a boat ramp or boat launch pursuant to MCL 324.30101 *et seq.*

Important Lake Publication!

Michigan Lake & Stream Associations, Inc. (ML&SA) is pleased to continue to offer its publication "*Michigan Lake Associations – The Nuts and Bolts*" authored by Grand Rapids attorney Cliff Bloom (legal counsel for *The Michigan Riparian* magazine, ML&SA, and the Michigan Waterfront Alliance). This publication is a well-written, easily understood manual, which includes everything you ever wanted to know about Michigan lake associations. Topics in the booklet include how to form and maintain a lake association, conducting meetings, lobbying local governments, weed treatments, special assessment districts, dues, statutory lake boards, and many other association and waterfront issues.

ML&SA is offering this publication at the incredibly low price of $15.00 plus $3.50 S/H (for a total of $18.50 each). If you order three or more copies, the price is $12.00 each plus $3.50 S/H (for a total of $15.50 each). Questions? Call the office at 989-831-5100.

To order, make payment to **Michigan Lake & Stream Associations** and mail it with the order form to:

MLSA
306 East Main Street
Stanton, Michigan 48888

Name (please print): _____

Address: _____
        Street or P.O. Box Number

_____
City   State   Zip Code

Email address: _____

Telephone number: _____

Please select:	Please select:
___1 book @ **$15.00** plus $3.50 S/H = $18.50 ___2 books @ **$15.00 ea.** plus $7.00 S/H = $37.00	___3 books @ **$12.00 ea.** plus $10.50 S/H = $46.50 ___4 books @ **$12.00 ea.** plus $14.00 S/H = $62.00 ************** Order additional books @ $15.50 including S/H ___books ordered @ $15.50 ea. $_____

304 East Main Street   Stanton, Michigan 48888
Phone: 989.831.5100
Email: info@mi-riparian.org   Web site: www.mi-riparian.org

Individual Subscription Order

☐New Subscriber   ☐ Renewal

Please print

Name_____Date_____

Address_____Phone (_____)_____

City _____State_____Zip_____

Email_____

Annual subscription is $14.00 per person for 4 issues per year—
WINTER (January) SPRING (April) SUMMER (July) FALL (October)

Annual subscription $14.00

Amount enclosed   _____

> Questions or change of address?
> Email: info@mi-riparian.org

Please allow 4-6 weeks for your first issue to arrive

Mail subscription order along with your payment to:

The Michigan Riparian
304 E. Main Street
Stanton, MI 48888

Devoted to the management and wise use of Michigan's lakes and streams
Keep informed to protect your lake—Subscribe to The Michigan Riparian

Office Use		
Check No._____	Date Rec'd._____	1st Issue Date _____/_____/_____
Amount_____	Rec'd By_____	Last Issue Date _____/_____/_____

www 11

Attachment N
MICHIGAN WATER-FRONT ALLIANCE MEMBERSHIP APPLICATION

_____ Annual dues for individual membership in the Michigan Waterfront Alliance ($50 per year)

_____ Dues for associations ($100 per year)

_____ Commercial, association and individual donations are also needed and appreciated ($200 per year).

Name: _____

(Please print)

Address: _____

City: _____ State: _____ Zip: _____

Email: _____

Lake/Stream Association: _____

Make Checks Payable to:

    Michigan Waterfront Alliance

Send Dues and Contributions to:

    Michigan Waterfront Alliance
    PO Box 369
    Fenton, Michigan 48430

Contacts: www.mwai.org or (989) 821-6661

Attachment O
LAKE CHARACTERISTIC CHECKLIST

1. All recreation lake (allows water skiing, motorized boats, personal watercraft, etc.) vs. a no-wake or quiet lake (electric motors only or no-wake speed) _____

2. Public (some type of public access, whether it be a public boat launch, park, road end, etc.) vs. private _____

3. Urban vs. rural _____

4. Large vs. small _____

5. Deep vs. shallow (also, is there a sharp drop off—safety issues) _____

6. Sandy beach and bottom vs. mucky bottom _____

7. Natural vs. artificial _____

8. High property values vs. medium property values vs. low property values _____

9. An existing cottage or house vs. a vacant lakefront lot _____

10. Protective local zoning regulations vs. inadequate or no zoning regulations _____

11. Commute time (to work, to be present on weekends, etc.)
     _____

12. Artificially-maintained lake level (via a dam, augmentation well, etc.)
     vs. natural lake levels _____

13. Public sewer or private septic? _____

14. Public water or private wells? _____

15. Municipal or association treatment of aquatic weeds vs. no aquatic
     weed treatment program _____

16. Subject to deed restrictions or no deed restrictions _____

17. A strong lake association vs. a weak lake association vs. no lake
     association _____

18. High property taxes vs. modest property taxes vs. low property taxes
     _____

19. Presence of a special assessment district _____

20. Quality of the lake water _____

21. Services and other recreational opportunities in the area vs. none
     _____

22. Ability to get your large boat in and out of the water seasonally (the
     presence of a public or private boat ramp) _____

23. Type of local government (city, village, or township) _____

24. Extensive local government services vs. few local government
     services _____

25. Quality of the lake as a fishing lake (during both the summer season
     and in the winter) _____

26. Quality of the lake neighborhood where the waterfront property is
     located _____

27. Quality of the school district _____

28. Availability of various utilities (Internet, telephone, natural gas,
     electric, etc.) _____

29. Proximity to negative uses (funnel developments, landfills, airports,
     mining operations, sewage plants, expressways or heavily-traveled
     roads, industrial uses, etc.) _____

30. Proximity to a farm (this can be a plus due to the positive aesthetics of a farm and lack of nearby residential neighbors, but it can also be a problem due to odors, water runoff, etc. that is protected by the Michigan Right to Farm Act, being MCL 286.471 *et seq.*) _____

31. Area crime rate _____

32. Distance to and quality of the local fire department _____

33. Cost of homeowner's insurance for the area _____

34. Will flood insurance be necessary? _____

35. Proximity of sidewalks, regional trailways, walkways, etc. _____

36. The existence of local government ordinances that could impact the lake (fertilizer bans, dock regulations, water skiing and high-speed boating-hour regulations, etc.) _____

37. Seasonal or year-round neighborhood _____

38. The presence of lake access devices on the property or nearby (parallel or perpendicular road ends, easements, parks, walkways, etc.) _____

39. Child-friendly neighborhood vs. seniors or empty nesters _____

40. Which "side" of the lake? (east shore, north shore, etc.) _____

41. "Natural" parcels vs. well-manicured neighborhoods _____

42. Is the property subject to high winds? Direct sunlight? Flooding? Erosion? _____